MW00812640

I sincerely hope...that the gardens and grounds will of themselves be a country place museum where visitors may enjoy as I have, not only the flowers, trees and shrubs, but the sunlit meadows, shady wood paths, and the peace and great calm of a country place which has been loved and taken care of for three generations.

Henry Francis du Pont

WINTERTHUR MUSEUM, GARDENS & LIBRARY

Jana Milbocker

The Garden Tourist's
MID-ATLANTIC

A Guide to 90 Beautiful Historic and Public Gardens

Enchanted Gardens

Cover: Hershey Gardens, Hershey, PA
Above: Untermyer Gardens, Yonkers, NY *Right:* Chanticleer, Wayne, PA

Copyright ©2024 by Jana Milbocker

All rights reserved.
No part of this book may be reproduced or transmitted in any form or by any means, electronic or mechanical, including photocopying, recording, or by any information storage and retrieval system, without written permission from the author, except for the inclusion of brief quotations in a review.

Published by Enchanted Gardens
For ordering information please contact
Enchanted Gardens, P.O. Box 6433, Holliston, MA 01746, 508-494-8768, thegardentourist@gmail.com

Cover and interior designed by Jana Milbocker. Photo credits appear on page 210.
Edited by Kathy Brown
Printed in U.S.A.

Publisher's Cataloging-in-Publication Data provided by Five Rainbows Cataloging Services
Names: Milbocker, Jana, author.
Title: The garden tourist's mid-Atlantic : a guide to 90 beautiful historic and public gardens / Jana Milbocker.
Description: Holliston, MA : Enchanted Gardens, 2024. | Includes index.
Identifiers: LCCN 2024902220 (print) | ISBN 978-0-9988335-5-2 (paperback)
Subjects: LCSH: Gardens--Hudson River Valley (N.Y. and N.J.)--Guidebooks. | Hudson River Valley (N.Y. and N.J.)--Guidebooks. | Gardens--Middle Atlantic States--Guidebooks. | Garden tours. | Tourism--Environmental aspects. | BISAC: GARDENING / Regional / Middle Atlantic (DC, DE, MD, NJ, NY, PA) | TRAVEL / United States / Northeast / Middle Atlantic (NJ, NY, PA) | GARDENING / Garden Design. | GARDENING / Reference.
Classification: LCC SB466.U65 H834 (print) | LCC SB466.U65 (ebook) | DDC 712.09747/3--dc23.
Library of Congress Control Number: 2024902220

First Edition

CONTENTS

List of Gardens by State

Chanticleer, Wayne, PA

Hershey Gardens, Hershey, PA

Winterthur, Wilmington, DE

Introduction

The Mid-Atlantic states of New York, New Jersey, Pennsylvania, and Delaware have a rich gardening history. With grand estates along the Hudson River, the du Pont family gardens in Delaware and Pennsylvania, and "America's Garden Capital" of the Philadelphia area, there are many wonderful gardens to visit in this region.

In addition to beautiful gardens, many properties offer art, history, and beautiful architecture. Art lovers will enjoy modern sculpture at Grounds for Sculpture and Kykuit, Medieval art at The Met Cloisters, and paintings of the Hudson River School at Olana. History and antique buffs will delight in the Gilded Age mansions of the Vanderbilt Estate and Nemours, the world-renowned collection of American decorative arts at Winterthur, and the political history of Springwood. Avid gardeners will be inspired at Longwood Gardens, Chanticleer, New York Botanical Garden, Stonecrop, Morris Arboretum & Gardens, and Mt. Cuba Center, to name a few. These gardens feature outstanding plant collections and design concepts.

The Mid-Atlantic region is seeing an exciting resurgence in garden creation and restoration. The Delaware Botanic Gardens at Pepper Creek is the brainchild of locals who believed that southern Delaware needed a horticultural destination. New Jersey's Greenwood Gardens and other grand estates such as Untermyer Gardens, Lyndhurst, and Wave Hill have recently been restored to their former glory with the generous and enthusiastic support of private donors. Other historic gardens such as Duke Farms and Stoneleigh have charted a new course by developing beautiful and sustainable gardens of native plants for the 21st century.

This book is a virtual garden tour of these diverse gardens, from large formal landscapes to small private oases. Some were designed by renowned landscape architects, while others evolved over time without a formal plan. Some have an educational mission, while others are designed for pleasure, healing, or quiet appreciation of the natural world. I have also included several specialty nurseries and private gardens that will open to the public by appointment. Gardens truly are reflections of their creators. This guide includes an introduction to some of the extraordinary individuals who took their passion for horticulture and created a retreat that others can enjoy for years to come.

Special thanks to my dear friends Susan Bonthron and Susan Mitrano and my daughter Katrina Milbocker for introducing me to many of the gardens in this book. I hope that this guide will inspire you, whether you're a gardener or a traveler. Enjoy your visits to the many enchanting gardens in the Mid-Atlantic. Happy touring!

Jana Milbocker

3 **5** **15**

NEW YORK
Suggested Daily Itineraries

Yaddo Garden, Saratoga Springs (1)
Lunch–Boca Bistro, Saratoga Springs

Clermont State Historic Site,
Germantown (3)
Lunch–Gaskins, Germantown
Blithewood (4) and Montgomery Place,
(5) Annandale-on-the-Hudson

Bellefield, Hyde Park (6)
Springwood, Hyde Park (7)
Lunch–Culinary Institute, Hyde Park
Vanderbilt Estate, Hyde Park (8)

Locust Grove Estate, Poughkeepskie (11)
Adams Fairacre Farm, Poughkeepsie (13)
Lunch–Brasserie 292, Poughkeepsie
Vassar College Shakespeare Garden,
Poughkeepsie (12)

Caramoor, Katonah (18)
Lunch–Blue Dolphin, Katonah
Lasdon Park, Arboretum & Veterans
Memorial, Katonah (17)

Boscobel, Garrison (16)
*Lunch–Brasserie Le Bouchon, Cold
Spring*
Stonecrop, Cold Spring (15)

Kykuit, Pocantico Hills (19)
Lunch–Sweetgrass Grill, Tarrytown
Lyndhurst, Tarrytown (20)

New York Botanical Garden, Bronx (25)
Lunch–New York Botanical Garden Café
Wave Hill, Bronx (24)

Heather Garden, New York (23)
The Met Cloisters, New York (22)
Lunch–Trie Cafe, The Met Cloisters
Untermyer Gardens, Yonkers(21)

NEW YORK

Yaddo Garden

312 Union Ave., Saratoga Springs, NY 12866
518-584-0746
yaddo.org

AREA: 10 acres
HOURS: June–Oct.: Mon.–Thurs. 11–4, Sat.–Sun. 9–1;
closed on Travers Day
ADMISSION: Free
EVENTS: Yoga, wellness, and other programs

In 1881, financier, philanthropist, and art patron Spencer Trask and his wife Katrina, a writer, purchased a country estate in Saratoga Springs that their daughter Christina named "Yaddo." They built a 55-room Queen Anne Revival mansion and welcomed artists and writers to visit.

Spencer presented the 10-acre garden to his wife as a gift in 1899. Although the Trasks consulted landscape architects and gardening references, the garden's ultimate design was theirs. The mansion's lower lawn features a large pool with fountains and marble statuary. A wrought-iron gate inscribed with the name Yaddo leads to the gardens, which occupy two terraces divided by a 180-foot

long rose-covered pergola, and feature beautiful fountains. The lower terrace with its rose garden is formal in style, and reflects the Italian gardens the Trasks had seen abroad. Four oblong beds bloom with more than 300 roses each. Adorning the garden are Italian marble statues of the Four Seasons, and a statue of a youth, *Christalan* sculpted by William Ordway Partridge as a memorial to the Trask children. The sundial overlooking the garden is inscribed with the poem "Time Is" by the Trask's friend Henry Van Dyke.

The upper terrace is a woodland rock garden, a style that came into fashion in the late 19th century. This shade garden, with its 100-year-old pines, features pools made of dolomite stone that are connected by a water rill. A large pyramidal pile of stones in the upper pool has a single spray fountain that fills the garden with the sound of falling water. Colorful perennials surround the lower pond.

Left without immediate heirs by the premature deaths of all four of their children, the Trasks bequeathed their fortune and estate to the establishment of a residency program for artists. The Corporation of Yaddo was founded in 1900 with the intent of providing "rest and refreshment [for] authors, painters, sculptors, musicians, and other artists both men and women, few in number but chosen for their creative gifts." The estate has welcomed many notable artists and writers including Truman Capote, Aaron Copland, Langston Hughes, and Sylvia Plath. The Trasks also stipulated that the gardens should remain open to the public free of charge, as they were during their lifetime. The gardens are maintained by the Yaddo Gardens Association, a group of dedicated volunteers.

Olana State Historic Site

5720 State Route 9G, Hudson, NY 12534
518-751-0344
olana.org

AREA: 250 acres

HOURS: Grounds: Daily 8–sunset. House: May–Oct.: Tues.–Sun. 10-3:45

ADMISSION: Landscape: free; House: $20 and up

AMENITIES: 🏞️ 👪 🎫

EVENTS: Landscape tour, lectures, youth programs

Frederic Edwin Church was a renowned painter, world traveler, self-taught architect and landscape designer. The home that he built for his family in the Hudson River Valley is considered his tour-de-force, surrounded by a living landscape painting.

Church was born in 1826 and studied with Thomas Cole in his Catskill, New York, studio from 1844 to 1846. The two artists went on sketching sojourns in the Berkshires, the Catskills, and in Hudson, across the river from Cole's studio. After his studies with Cole, Church moved to New York City and became a rising star in the art world with his vivid landscape paintings. His panoramic canvases conveyed the expansionist, optimistic worldview of mid-19th-century America and were renowned for their meticulous atmospheric and botanical detail. Church's legacy is alive today as the best-known artist of the Hudson River School.

At the height of his career in 1860, Church purchased 126 acres of hardscrabble farmland on a hillside near Hudson. The land had been cleared for farming but had beautiful views of the Hudson River. Church had a unique vision for Olana. He wanted to create both a profitable working farm and an inspiring ornamental landscape. Over time the landscape became Church's principal artistic medium. He acquired additional land parcels with views to the Catskills and the Taconic Hills, and he began creating a picturesque-style landscape that was popularized by Andrew Jackson Downing. This included the planting of native woodlands, with thousands of maples, birches, hickories, hemlocks, chestnuts, pines, and oaks. The trees were used to create dense woods, frame beautiful views, or screen out buildings.

Church built five miles of carriage roads on his property to provide dramatic views of meadows, mountains, and the farm. Some followed the site's undulating landscape, while others required blasting with dynamite. He also transformed a swampy area into a 10-acre hand-dug lake. Excavating the muck to form a lake took 20 years, but the nutritious soil was used to establish and feed new plantings. The lake was both functional and ornamental. It provided a source of water for the property and a recreational area for boating, skating, and fishing. It was also a design feature that echoed the shape of Inbocht Bay several miles downriver.

The focal point of the landscape was the grand mansion that Church designed and built in 1872. Sited on the highest point of the property 500 feet above the Hudson River, the house offers sublime views of the landscape below. Church was inspired by his travels in Europe and the Middle East, and he worked closely with architect Calvert Vaux to create a truly unique home. With its towers, fanciful windows and porches, decorative brickwork, patterned slate roof, and stenciling, the house is an incredible work of art. Be sure to take a tour of

the interior, as it combines Middle Eastern motifs with Victorian decor and showcases Church's beautiful landscape paintings. The house itself became Church's masterpiece, one that he continued to refine until his death in 1900.

The approach to the house was carefully designed so that the mansion would remain mysteriously hidden until visitors were close by. Landscaping around the home was kept simple with only ornamental trees. Even the small cutting garden was situated below a retaining wall so that it would not detract from the views of the house and the naturalistic landscape.

Clermont State Historic Site

1 Clermont Ave., Germantown, NY 12526
518-537-4240
parks.ny.gov/historic-sites

AREA: 500 acre estate

HOURS: Grounds: daily 8:30–sunset; house: Thurs.–Sun. 11–4

ADMISSION: Gardens: free; house $7, parking $5

AMENITIES:

EVENTS: Sheep & Wool Showcase, Independence Day, lectures, concerts, other events

Clermont was the Hudson River seat of New York's politically and socially prominent Livingston family. Seven generations left their imprint on the site's architecture, interiors, and landscape. The most renowned member of the family was Chancellor Robert R. Livingston, an active patriot during the Revolution. He was a member of the Committee of Five that drafted the Declaration of Independence, wrote the New York Constitution, and served as the nation's first Secretary for Foreign Affairs. After the war he administered the oath of office to George Washington, and led the negotiations for the Louisiana Purchase. He was also co-inventor of the first commercially viable steamboat.

The gardens and grounds at Clermont are in the process of being restored to the 1930s, when John and Alice Livingston were the last private owners of the estate. Alice arrived at Clermont as a bride in 1908 and developed four main gardens at the estate: the South Spring Garden, with its view of the Hudson River; the Upper Garden, which provided cut flowers for the house; the 60-by-30-foot walled flower garden with symmetrical parterres; and the wilderness garden with its fish pond. The formal walled garden was inspired by the family's six-year sojourn in Italy, providing cultural education for their daughters, Honoria and Janet. It contains a fine collection of hellebores, which were Livingston's favorite spring flowers. "It is a great event with us when they arrive, and usually I place the flowers with some sprigs of boxwood, floating in a turquoise bowl," Alice wrote in her journal.

"I am such a sucker for spring. I took a short walk in the garden this week, and my heart went all a-flutter to see nodding snowdrops, the magnolias just starting to bloom, and the daffodils up in full force."
—Alice Livingston

The adjoining wilderness garden was meant to contrast the formality of the walled garden.

The Upper Cutting Garden is planted with perennials and contains the remains of a greenhouse that had been used to grow vegetables, roses, and flowers. Peonies were favorite flowers for bouquets for the house, and many heirloom peonies remain. Alice introduced her daughters to gardening early. She gave each a garden plot next to the cutting garden, and the garden shed became their playhouse. Both daughters became gardeners as adults.

In the late 1920s, Alice enhanced Clermont's spring floral display by expanding the Lilac Walk, which had been originally planted in the early 1800s. She added dozens of traditional varieties and fancy French hybrids, as well as other flowering trees and shrubs. Early May is an excellent time to visit Clermont, when the scent of lilacs perfumes the air.

During World War II, Alice, then a widow, moved into the gardener's cottage, and lived there for the remainder of her life, tending her beloved gardens. In 1962 the house and property were transferred to the State of New York. In addition to the gardens, Clermont's trails feature some of the best bird watching in the region.

Blithewood

Bard College, Campus Road, Annandale-on-the-Hudson, NY 12504
845-752-5323
bard.edu/arboretum/about/blithewood/

AREA: 0.5 acre garden
HOURS: Grounds: daily dawn–dusk
ADMISSION: Free

Blithewood is one of several important Hudson River estates that form the Bard College campus. It features a Beaux Arts mansion (now the Levy Economics Institute) with a formal Italianate walled garden in a grand setting—130 feet above the Hudson River overlooking a panorama of the Catskill Mountains.

The garden was constructed in 1903 for Captain Andrew Zabriskie, a real-estate tycoon and captain of the National Guard, to accompany his Georgian-style mansion. Francis Hoppin designed the elegant space in the Beaux-Arts style popular during the Gilded Age. Wide marble steps lead from the mansion to a 15,000 square-foot architectural sunken garden with gravel paths on geometric axes, symmetrical beds, a central water feature, statuary, and marble ornaments. The walls create a peaceful green room, and a copper-roofed gazebo flanked by two wisteria-covered pergolas

frames a majestic view of the river.

Capt. Zabriskie's wife Frances was an avid horticulturist. Historically the garden had clipped evergreens and plantings of tulips, daffodils, lavender, lilacs, roses, iris, wisteria, peonies, and annuals. Today's plantings are inspired by the historic palette, but include contemporary plant choices as well: grasses, hydrangeas, hardy geraniums, clematis, and a wide range of other perennials. Bard College and the Garden Conservancy are collaborating on desperately needed repairs to the historic structures and hardscape.

The lawn areas surrounding the mansion offer gorgeous views, with picnic tables and lawn chairs that invite you to linger. The grounds contain many important and venerable tree specimens, including a former New York State Champion red maple that is estimated to be more than 300 years old. The entire 550-acre Bard campus is an arboretum landscaped with many small pocket gardens, each with its own theme: a woodland garden, Japanese garden, Elizabethan knot garden, meditation garden, and more. Self-guided walking tour brochures of the campus arboretum are available at bard.edu/arboretum/visit.

Montgomery Place

Bard College, Campus Road, Annandale-on-the-Hudson, NY 12504
845-752-5323
bard.edu/arboretum/about/montgomeryplace/

AREA: 380 acres

HOURS: Grounds: daily dawn-dusk

ADMISSION: Free

AMENITIES:

Purchased by Bard College in 2016, Montgomery Place was, for nearly two centuries, the summer retreat of the Livingston family, whose members were prominent in politics, the military, and in New York social circles. Renowned architects, landscape designers, and horticulturists created an elegant country estate with farmland, manicured lawns, woodlands, and gardens overlooking the Hudson River and the Catskill Mountains.

The gardens at Montgomery Place were shaped by women of several generations. Janet Livingston Montgomery built the original house in 1805. She was a passionate botanist, and established a commercial nursery for fruit trees, shrubs, berries, and seeds. In the late 1800s, landscape designer Andrew Jackson Downing created plans for an arboretum, walking paths, and elaborate flower gardens for Cora Montgomery.

Today, the gardens reflect the period between 1925 and 1945 and the influence of Violetta

White Delafield. Her husband General John Ross Delafield inherited Montgomery Place, and Violetta saw the property's potential, and need, for new gardens. An accomplished horticulturist and mycologist who studied with some of the key botany professors of the time, Violetta published three scientific monographs, and several mushroom species were named after her. The late 19th century witnessed a surge of women into the botanical field, particularly on the East and West coasts. Violetta applied her scientific approach to Montgomery Place: she did an inventory of the flora and commissioned a census of native plants on the property. She also applied her passion and creativity to developing the gardens.

The Delafields first concentrated on the gardens surrounding the mansion. They terraced the slope behind the house toward the river, and planted flowers along the terrace balustrades. They also installed a naturalistic pond surrounded by white dogwoods at the base of the slope to foreshorten the visual distance to the Hudson River. They restored the trails and carriage lanes, and planted unusual understory trees such as Kousa dogwood, silverbell, and sourwood.

While respectful of the historic landscape she had inherited, Violetta had her own ideas and was influenced by American landscape designers of the day. One of the trends at the time was to create themed pocket gardens. Pocket gardens allowed Violetta to create a variety of different gardens while maintaining the overall naturalistic style of the property. She installed an elaborate alpine garden with a frog pond that later morphed into a "wild garden" and is glorious in spring with the blooms of trilliums, trout lilies, bloodroot, ferns, and thousands of bulbs. She also added the peaceful "green garden" with an elliptical reflecting pool enclosed by hemlocks and rhododendrons.

Violetta added a potting shed and greenhouse for starting annuals and growing cacti and other succulents. She redesigned an old rose garden near the potting shed, and planted each bed in a different color scheme. She also planted borders of the 'Livingston' rose that she had found in her predecessor's kitchen garden, as a tribute to her family (actually 'Jacques Cartier'). A Colonial Revival herb garden with a central sundial was added next to the rose garden. Except for the expansive vegetable and cutting gardens, Violetta's gardens exist today and are restored to their 1920s appearance.

Bellefield

4097 Albany Post Rd., Hyde Park, NY 12538
845-229-9115 x2023
beatrixfarrandgardenhydepark.org

AREA: 2 acres of gardens
HOURS: Daily 7 am–sunset
ADMISSION: Free
EVENTS: Gardening workshops, design lectures

Adjacent to the National Park Service building, the Bellefield garden is almost hidden from view on the grounds of Springwood, Franklin D. Roosevelt National Historic Site. The mansion was the former home of Thomas and Sarah Newbold, who hired Thomas' cousin Beatrix Farrand in 1912 to design their garden. Farrand designed a whole plan for the property, which included a series of three interconnected walled gardens descending from the elegant 18th century house, as well as a rose garden, a lilac and fruit-tree allée, a boxwood parterre, and a kitchen garden.

The Newbold family donated the property to the National Park Service in the 1970s, and over time the gardens disappeared due to neglect. In 1994 a volunteer group was formed to restore the walled gardens, which you can visit on the property today. Although the walls and bed outlines of the garden were still in place, most of the plantings, as well as the original planting plans, were long gone. The walls and gates were repaired and replaced using Farrand's original sketches, and the garden was replanted based on planting plans she had created for other properties.

The Bellefield walled gardens are unique for several reasons. Farrand employed an interesting perspective illusion by making each garden smaller than the one next to it. This makes the garden appear longer than it actually is.

Farrand's signature design technique was the use of color-themed borders in her designs, and this scheme was adapted at Bellefield. The flower beds are planted in four color schemes: pink, white, mauve/purple, and blush/cream/gray. Each border displays a beautiful progression of bloom through the growing season. To enhance the illusion of a long perspective, bright colors—pinks, blues, and purples—are featured in the beds closest to the house, while lighter colors—whites, creams, and silvers—are used at the far end of the garden.

Beatrix Farrand

The best time to see Bellefield is in the spring and early summer, when the bulbs and perennials are in peak flower. The pink border's peonies are survivors from the original garden, and are flanked by foxgloves, phlox, and poppies in spring, followed by astilbes and 'Stargazer' lilies in summer. The white border's spring blooms include daffodils, camassias, tulips, columbines and cosmos, followed by acteas, phloxes, anemones, and hostas. The mauve/purple border is filled with early crocus, irises, phloxes, verbenas, sea lavenders, and balloon flowers. The blush/cream/gray border displays dramatic lilies, plume poppies, and

acanthus, underplanted with lamb's ears, santolinas, and artemisias. Planting plans and plant lists for the color-themed borders are available on the website. The stone walls are covered with wisteria, akebia, trumpet vine, and honeysuckle.

Plans are currently underway to restore the Wild Garden that originally framed the walled garden. This garden would illustrate another aspect of Farrand's design aesthetic and incorporate many native species that Farrand used in her designs.

Springwood Estate

114 Estates Ln., Hyde Park, NY 12538
845-229-9115
nps.gov/places/springwood.htm

AREA: 265 acres total, gardens are about 5 acres

HOURS: Grounds: daily 7–6; house: daily 9:30–4, closed on holidays

ADMISSION: Grounds: free; entire estate: $10

AMENITIES: 🏛️ 🚻 🎫

EVENTS: Holiday Open House, hikes, exhibits

Springwood was the beloved home of Franklin Delano Roosevelt, the 32nd President of the United States. It was his birthplace, a haven that he returned to as often as possible, his political headquarters where he entertained numerous dignitaries, and his burial place. The gardens and 265 acres of woodlands and meadows on the Hudson River were an integral part of Roosevelt's life and nurtured a life-long interest in nature and the environment.

The original estate, consisting of a 15-room house on one square mile of property, was bought by FDR's father, James Roosevelt, in 1866. Springwood was a working farm with a large vegetable garden, fields producing corn and hay, and experimental forestry plantations. The roads connecting outbuildings and various landscape features on the estate were heavily tree-lined, creating dense canopies throughout.

When asked his profession, FDR—whose titles included Governor of New York, Assistant Secretary of the Navy, and President of the United States—would respond: "I am a tree grower." Visiting the Chicago World's Fair in 1893, the young Roosevelt was attracted to the exhibit of trees native to New York State. From that time on, he studied and practiced the arts of planting, transplanting, pruning, watering, and spacing trees. Between 1911 and Roosevelt's death in 1945, more than 400,000 trees were planted on the Springwood estate. As president, FDR was responsible for the planting of 3 billion trees in the United States—with hundreds of thousands of those creating shelter belts to prevent another Dust Bowl.

The Rose Garden and Home Garden were key features of Springwood, and were supervised by FDR's mother, Sara Roosevelt. FDR sited his Presidential Library so that he could view the Home Garden from his office window, and so he would pass through the Rose Garden on his way back to the house in the evening. The Rose Garden contains 30 beds of hybrid tea and shrub roses in shades of pink, red, and white; an exquisite collection of historic peonies; and beds artfully planted with summer annuals. Franklin and Eleanor Roosevelt are buried there with a simple monument marking the gravesite.

The two-acre Home Garden—a large fruit and vegetable garden—was central to the life of the family. In addition to vegetables, it contained apple and pear trees, as well as an apiary that provided pollinators for the fruit trees and honey for the family. This garden was recently restored and is planted with many of the vegetable and fruit varieties grown by the Roosevelts. It exhibits numerous vegetable growing techniques.

The Presidential Library and Val-Kil, Eleanor Roosevelt's residence, have their own tickets and visiting schedule.

Vanderbilt Mansion

119 Vanderbilt Park Rd., Hyde Park, NY 12538
845-229-7770
home.nps.gov/vama/index.htm

AREA: 211 acres total, garden is about 3 acres
HOURS: Grounds: daily dawn–dusk; house: daily 9–5
ADMISSION: Grounds: free; house: $10
AMENITIES:
EVENTS: Holiday Open House, lectures, exhibits

In 1895 Cornelius Vanderbilt's grandson Frederick and his wife, Louise, bought the Hudson River estate known as Hyde Park to use as their spring and fall country home. Frederick was a quiet man, active in the business of directing 22 railroads, while Louise was a wealthy socialite. They built a Neoclassical Beaux Arts mansion furnished with European antiques, and outfitted with all the latest innovations: electricity, indoor plumbing, and central heating. The grounds were enhanced with a pavilion, coach house, new bridges, power station, boat docks, railroad station, and extensive landscaping. The final cost totaled $2.25 million, or $82 million in today's dollars.

The Vanderbilts were part of a new wave of urban elite that moved to the Hudson River Valley to enjoy relaxed country living, the sporting life, farming, and outdoor recreation. Lavish weekend parties included horseback riding, golf, tennis, and swimming, followed by formal dinners and dancing. Hyde Park was a self-sustaining estate, providing food and flowers for the family's needs

there and at their other homes. When not hosting guests, the Vanderbilts strolled through the gardens and greenhouses twice daily and visited their farm.

The grounds had been shaped by several previous owners with horticultural interests. In the early 1800s, Dr. Samuel Bard planted exotic plants and trees in the European Picturesque style. The next owner, Dr. David Hosack, had a passion for botany and established the first formal gardens on the estate, as well as extensive greenhouses to hold his exotic plants. He also hired André Parmentier to design the landscape. Roads, bridges, and lawns were laid out to complement natural features, while large areas were left wild. Today, much of Parmentier's original design continues to be admired for its grace and beauty. In the late 1800s, owner Walter Langdon, Jr., laid out the formal gardens and built the gardener's cottage, tool house, and garden walls, which remain and are in use today.

A large, formal garden was common to most Gilded Age estates. Frederick had a horticulture degree from Yale University, and established the grand, Italian-style, terraced garden. The upper garden features formal flower beds, while the lower garden exhibits a mélange of curvilinear shapes—crescents, hearts, and circular beds, all

planted with bright annuals. An esplanade of cherry trees leads to a walled perennial garden, which opens up to a long reflecting pool and a brick loggia decorated with the statue of an odalisque in mid-dance. The path continues to a two-tier rose garden with a charming summerhouse.

After Frederick's death in 1938, the federal government purchased the estate, thanks to the intervention of President Franklin Roosevelt. While the grounds, landscaping, and buildings were preserved, there were no funds to maintain the gardens, which suffered years of neglect. Today the landscape is restored to its 1930s appearance, thanks to the Frederick W. Vanderbilt Garden Association—a group of volunteers who have worked tirelessly to bring the gardens to their former glory. The walled gardens were replanted with 3,200 perennials and 2,000 roses. An additional 6,500 annuals are planted every year. The restored gravel paths, shady arbors, ornate statues, and bubbling fountains give the visitor a glimpse of life in the Gilded Age.

Wethersfield Estate & Garden

257 Pugsley Hill Rd., Amenia, NY 12501
845-373-8037
wethersfield.org

AREA: 13 acres of gardens
HOURS: Garden: June–mid-Oct.: Fri.–Sun. 12–5
ADMISSION: Garden: $15; House: $10
AMENITIES:

Nestled in 1,000 acres of beautiful rolling hills in New York's Dutchess County, Wethersfield is considered one of the best examples of a classic Italian Renaissance garden in America.

Wethersfield was built as a summer residence by Chauncey Deveraux Stillman (1907-1989), an heir to one of America's great family banking fortunes. Chauncey was a true Renaissance man, with interests in yachting, art, sculpture, architecture, religion, farming, wildlife, horticulture, and horses. In fact it was the Millbrook Hunt that brought him to Dutchess County, where he was struck by the amazing views and farming potential of the land. In 1937 Chauncey purchased two abandoned farms, built his Georgian Colonial residence, and expanded the property over the next 50 years.

In 1947 Chauncey commissioned landscape architect Evelyn N. Poehler to design a swimming pool. The commission grew into the design of a three-acre traditional Italian Renaissance Garden and a

ten-acre Wilderness Garden whose design evolved over the next 25 years. Italian Renaissance gardens are known for their architectural design with a strong central axis, allées of trees, clipped hedges, and enclosed garden rooms. Pairs of shrubs, trees, statues, or urns frame views and entrances. These are green gardens, with flowers used primarily as accents. Poehler used a series of terraces to divide the sloping property into formal garden rooms. The Lower Terrace is the main axis of the garden, framed by clipped yews and weeping beeches. On a rise above, the Belvedere offers stunning views of rolling hills and woodlands that surround the formal gardens. A solid shale wall topped by a stone balustrade features a niche enclosing a cupid fountain with plantings of sedums, campanulas, and other delicate flowers spilling from the stones. The Upper Terrace forms the Peacock Walk, with a cage of these colorful birds at one end.

The Lower Terrace features a beautiful oval reflecting pool, which was originally the swimming pool that launched the design of the garden. A perpendicular axis here is formed by the 190-foot long allée of tall arborvitae. The allée leads to a fountain with a green and gold naiad, or water nymph, created by sculptor Carl Milles.

Adjacent to the house is the Inner Garden that is enclosed by the house, a beech tunnel, and a walled knot garden. A grape arbor creates an extension of the dining room and was used for outdoor lunches. The Persian-style rill brings the soothing sound of water to this lovely courtyard. Borders of perennials and annuals frame the keyhole lawn. Curved steps lead to the Victorian-style knot gardens and the summerhouse.

The Palladian Arch leads to the Wilderness Garden, a woodland garden with carriage drives and trails that weave through stands of trees underplanted with rhododendrons, mountain laurels, and ferns, and accented with statuary.

Innisfree Garden

362 Tyrrel Rd., Millbrook, NY 12545
845-677-8000
innisfreegarden.org

AREA: 185 acres

HOURS: May–Oct.: Wed.–Fri. 10–5. Check website for additional hours

ADMISSION: $10

AMENITIES:

EVENTS: Guided garden tours, nature walks, special programs

Innisfree garden is the result of a deep friendship and collaboration among three people: owners Walter and Marion Beck and landscape designer Lester Collins. In the late 1920s, artist Walter and his avid gardener wife, Marion, bought their country residence, which they named Innisfree, and began to study garden design and philosophy. Walter discovered the work of eighth-century Chinese poet, painter, and gardener Wang Wei. Studying scroll paintings of Wang's famed garden, Walter was drawn to the carefully defined, inwardly focused gardens sited within a larger, naturalistic landscape that Wang created. Wang's technique influenced centuries of Chinese and Japanese garden design, and the gardens of Innisfree. Drawing on Wang's approach, the Becks created vignettes in the garden, which Walter called "cup gardens," incorporating rocks from the site with trees and plantings. Relating these to one another and to the landscape as a whole was the role of Lester Collins.

The Becks met Collins early in 1938 and began their creative collaboration. Collins was one of the most influential designers and educators of his era. A modernist and scholar who travelled and studied extensively in Asia, the Middle East, and Africa, Collins became Dean of Landscape Architecture at Harvard University. In his 20-year association with the Becks, Collins was able to create a magical garden that brought the Becks' "cup gardens" into a unified whole.

Having no children, the Becks decided to endow a foundation for the "study of garden art at Innisfree" that would make it into a public garden. Collins became the estate's manager, orchestrated its transition to a public garden, and continued to design and expand the landscape according to his and the Becks' vision. As funds allowed, he cleared portions of the densely wooded site, carefully editing existing vegetation to leave magnificent trees and swaths of natives, such as blueberries, irises, and ferns. He created the first route around the lake; added new cup gardens; designed such memorable water features as the Mist, the Water Sculpture, the Air Spring, and the Fountain Jet; sculpted fanciful berms like those along the Entrance Drive, and added new plantings of native and Asian varieties to create a garden that is natural, unpretentious, and sustainable. His involvement with the garden continued for 55 years until his death in 1993. Today, the garden is run by the Innisfree Foundation.

Innisfree is a naturalistic stroll garden in which the hand of the designer is almost invisible. The design comes from the study of the natural site. The gardens at Innisfree are based around the 40-acre lake framed by wooded hills and rocky

cliffs. Rocks are an important element—from stone walls and staircases to single monolithic stones that create strong verticals in the landscape. Most of the stones were collected on the property and carefully placed in their current location. Dramatic water features provide movement and energy within the garden. Innisfree is a work of art for all to experience. For gardeners, it also offers a time-tested model for creating poetic, resilient, biodiverse landscapes. It is a garden of quiet beauty, serenity, and contemplation.

Locust Grove Estate

2683 South Rd., Poughkeepsie, NY 12601
845-454-4500
www.lgny.org

AREA: 200 acres total; 3 acres of gardens
HOURS: Grounds: April–Dec. 10–5; mansion: May 1–Oct. 31, Fri.–Mon.10–5, weekends in December
ADMISSION: Grounds: free; mansion: $20
AMENITIES:
EVENTS: Peony sales, special events

The Locust Grove Estate was shaped by two families—the Morses and the Youngs. The Italianate-style villa was built in 1851 as a summer home for Samuel F. B. Morse. Although best known for inventing the telegraph and Morse code, Morse was an artist and lecturer at the National Academy of Design and an avid gardener. As an artist he was strongly influenced by romantic 19th century design, which advocated a painterly approach to the landscape, with natural groupings of plants and curving lines. Morse used the property's natural features to shape the drives and paths and to create views. Morse's legacy at Locust Grove includes the majestic old maples, beeches, ginkgos, and tulip poplars that frame vistas throughout the property. A museum pavilion exhibits Morse's artwork and early telegraph equipment.

William and Martha Young brought a new vision to Locust Grove when they purchased the estate in 1895. They acquired adjoining properties and built scenic carriage drives along the Hudson. Martha was an avid gardener with a passion for flowers. She expanded the formal gardens near the house, laid out long, straight flower borders, and planted a large collection of peonies, which continue to thrive today.

Martha's gardens have been preserved and augmented with additional plants since Locust Grove

opened to the public in 1979. Where possible, old varieties of perennials are used. Lavenders, rudbeckias, echinaceas, and hydrangeas have been added to create a long bloom season. Since annuals were popular in the early 1900s, they are planted in drifts of a single color combined with blocks of perennials and selected shrubs to create 'pictures' that are beautiful whether as a detail or as a 100-foot-long composition. The peonies create an amazing display in June, and a 75-foot-long border of dahlias adds color after the peonies have passed.

Near the house, the geometric flower beds and urns are bedded out in Victorian style with tulips in spring, and annuals such as coleus, marigolds, ferns, and castor beans in the summer. The kitchen garden has also been restored and exhibits fruits and vegetables that were grown on the estate. A group of dedicated volunteers helps maintain the gardens.

Vassar College Shakespeare Garden

124 Raymond Ave., Poughkeepsie, NY 12604
845-437-7000
vassar.edu

AREA: 1 acre
HOURS: Daily dawn–dusk
ADMISSION: Free

Vassar's Shakespeare Garden was founded on April 24, 1916, with the planting of pansies (the flower of thoughts) and flower seeds from Shakespeare's garden in Stratford-on-Avon, England. The ceremony commemorated the 300th anniversary of The Bard's death. As the second-oldest Shakespeare garden in the country, and the only one at a liberal arts college, it has a special place in Vassar's history. It combines the traditional approach of displaying plants used in Shakespeare's writings with Vassar's educational philosophy.

The Shakespeare Garden began as an integral part of the curriculum—a site for both scholarly research and hands-on learning. The garden was a collaborative and multidisciplinary project, researched and planted by the students and professors of Shakespeare and botany classes. From its earliest days, it was also used as an outdoor theater. The garden's creators reached out to involve alumni and the larger Vassar community. Throughout the decades, the community's donations of plants, funds, and labor made this a

uniquely Vassar garden.

Since its founding, the garden has undergone several revisions by faculty, students, and volunteers. The latest restoration in 2019 was spearheaded by renowned landscape architect and alumnus Ed Hollander. The goal of the renovation was to preserve the garden's most beloved features while making it more accessible and sustainable. Today, a wide central staircase descends through three curved terraces to a bluestone patio with a historic sundial overlooking Fonteyn Kill creek. Raised brick beds display plants mentioned in Shakespeare's writings as well as those that were grown in England in the 17th century. Since the climate in Poughkeepsie is very different than in England, Shakespearean plants are augmented with hardy natives. The three iconic statues found in the garden have been attributed to characters in Shakespeare's plays, but are actually from the college founder's Springside estate.

The first terrace is "Oberon's Bank," inspired by King Oberon's quote to his fairy messenger Puck in *A Midsummer Night's Dream*: "I know a bank where the wild thyme blows, Where oxlips and the nodding violet grows, Quite over-canopies with luscious woodbine, With sweet musk rose and with eglantine…." You will find these plants along with wormwood, centaurea montana, roses, and others. Violets were mentioned in many of Shakespeare's works and were prized for their perfume and early bloom time. Thyme was a symbol of sweetness, beloved by fairies and bees for its sweet scent and nectar. Woodbine (honeysuckle) was considered an emblem of affection and faithfulness. Eglantine is sweet briar, a sweet single rose popular in English cottage gardens.

The second terrace is "Thistles and Thorns," inspired by the Wars of the Roses. Here you will find a selection of Knock Out, musk, damask, and English roses underplanted with native grasses,

Siberian irises, and echinops. So universal is the love for the rose, that Shakespeare mentioned it at least 70 times in his plays and sonnets. The Wars of the Roses is the central theme of *Henry VI*, and Juliet proclaims, "That which we call a rose by any other name would smell as sweet," in Shakespeare's most memorable quote.

The bottom terrace is divided into sevaral sections: "Ophelia's Garland, Et Cetera" (flowers mentioned in multiple plays), "Lilies of All Kinds" from *The Winter's Tale*, and "A Sweeter Shade" from *Henry VI*. In Ophelia's Garland, fennel is the emblem of flattery, while columbine symbolizes forsaken lovers. Rosemary is best known for faithfulness and remembrance and as a culinary herb, but it was highly prized as a medicinal plant in Elizabethan England. With its strong smell and bitter taste, rue was the herb of repentance and used as a preventative against the plague. In other beds you will find daylilies, which symbolized purity; irises, the symbols for France; and several varieties of sweet-smelling dianthus (carnations and pinks), which Shakespeare called "the fairest flowers o' the season."

Adams Fairacre Farms

765 Dutchess Tpke., Poughkeepsie, NY 12603
845-454-4330
adamsfarms.com

HOURS: Mon.–Sat. 7 am–8 pm, Sun. 7 am–7 pm

AMENITIES: 👥 🏪 ✕

EVENTS: Annual Lawn & Garden Show in Feb.-March

OTHER LOCATIONS: Kingston, Middletown, Newburgh, Wappinger

Adams Fairacre Farms illustrates a new concept in shopping for the home and garden. It is like a Whole Foods and a premium garden center combined under one roof—a place where you can spend your entire Saturday morning shopping for all that you need. Adams began in 1919 as a roadside farm stand in Poughkeepsie run by Ralph A. Adams and his family. Today, it continues as a family-owned and operated business with five locations in the Hudson Valley, and a loyal following of customers.

On the site of the original Adams Farm, the family oversees five acres of greenhouses and a produc-

tion area where more than two million bedding plants are grown annually from seed, as well as 300,000 hardy perennials, 110,000 mums and 80,000 poinsettias. It's one of the most extensive selections of locally grown plants in the Hudson Valley. Adams has confidence in their plant stock—they offer a two-year guarantee on all their trees and shrubs. They also carry a wide array of unusual conifers, Japanese maples, and landscape-size trees of all types.

The indoor Garden Center offers everything from seeds and seed-starting accessories, to garden tools, bird food and houses, patio furniture, grills, and hydroponic supplies. The Tropical Greenhouse features houseplants, as well as seasonal decorations, flower baskets, and annuals. Each year in late February through early March, Adams hosts its own Annual Lawn & Garden Show. The landscaping crew designs and builds displays of walkways, ponds, and patios decorated with hundreds of flowering spring bulbs, annuals, trees, and shrubs in the greenhouses. Vendors, knowledgeable staff, and garden experts offer seminars, giveaways, and free raffles.

The original farm stand at Adams has been expanded into a mecca for foodies. In addition to beautiful fresh produce, there is a huge selection of prepared foods. Hosting a dinner party? You won't find a larger collection of international favorites under one roof, from coffees, cured meats, cheeses, and fancy chocolates, to gourmet pastas and sauces. Need a gift? Stroll over to the gift shop. Tired of shopping? You can enjoy a cup of coffee or an ice cream cone at the Poughkeepsie café. A trip to Adams is a trip to the nursery that the whole family can enjoy.

Stonecrop Gardens

81 Stonecrop Ln., Cold Spring, NY 10516
845-265-2000
www.stonecrop.org

AREA: 60 acres

HOURS: April–Oct.: Mon., Wed., Fri., Sat. & select Sundays 10–5

ADMISSION: $10

AMENITIES:

EVENTS: Plant sale, tours, workshops

Stonecrop Gardens has become a destination for gardeners and students of landscape design since it opened to the public in 1992. Its founder was Frank Cabot, a financier and self-taught horticulturist who began gardening to relieve the pressures of venture capitalism and ended up creating two of the most celebrated gardens in North America—Stonecrop Gardens in New York, and Les Quatre Vents in Quebec. He also founded the Garden Conservancy, and served as chairman of the New York Botanical Garden and advisor to botanic gardens in Brooklyn and Ontario.

Stonecrop began as a private garden in 1958, when Frank and his wife, Anne, built their home on 60 acres in the Hudson Highlands at an elevation of 1,100 feet. They began to garden on the rocky site and soon developed a passion for alpine plants. Since choice alpines were hard to come by, they started their own alpine mail-order nursery. Although the nursery no longer operates, you will see many alpines in Stonecrop's gardens and greenhouses, and some are available for sale.

Over the years the Cabots' garden grew to 12 acres. In the mid-1980s, they began planning for Stonecrop to become a public garden that would inspire and educate other gardeners. They engaged English horticulturist Caroline Burgess, who had studied at Kew Gardens and worked for Rosemary Verey. Under Burgess's direction, Stonecrop's gardens expanded in scope and diversity and now contain an encyclopedic collection of plants.

A visit to Stonecrop is a serious immersion in plants and design ideas. Plan to spend several hours with a plant list in hand. Some of the highlights include a cliff rock garden, woodland and water gardens, an enclosed English-style flower garden, and systematic order beds representing over 50 plant families.

Inspiration may be found in all seasons, from the spring show of bulbs and the explosion of color on the cliff ledge, to summer's profusion in the flower garden and the subtleties of fall foliage and fruit in the woodland. A 2,000-square-foot conservatory houses tender specimens, and display greenhouses feature alpines, tropicals, and succulents.

Orange County Arboretum

Thomas Bull Memorial Park, 15 Grove St., Montgomery, NY 12549
845-615-3830
orangecountyarboretum.org

AREA: 35 acres

HOURS: Daily dawn–dusk

ADMISSION: Free

AMENITIES:

EVENTS: Spring plant sale, holiday boutique, holiday lights, gardening and children's programs, Sept. 11 Memorial Ceremony

Nestled on 35 acres of former pasturelands in Thomas Bull Memorial Park, the Orange County Arboretum is an intimate horticultural sanctuary. The eight acres of formal gardens showcase beautiful bulb displays, water features, specimen trees, memorials, and plant collections.

Entering the arboretum you will find a courtyard with a long, wisteria-draped pergola, and raised flower beds that feature a beautiful display of daffodils, tulips, and grape hyacinths in spring. Flowering cherries and crabapples enhance the floral display. There are numerous benches where you can sit and enjoy the beautiful surroundings. In the summer the bulbs are replaced with colorful annuals and tropicals. From this courtyard, the Middle-Eastern inspired Rill leads to a pool with

gurgling fountains and a statue of Pan, the god of woods, fields, and flocks. Surrounding beds feature unusual tree specimens such as tri-color beech, sourwood, chestnut, and fastigiate oak.

The Alpine Garden is a beautifully designed space featuring huge boulders, standing stones, streams, and cascades. Vertical specimens of arborvitae, Colorado blue spruce, and juniper punctuate low plantings of prostrate conifers, sedums, grasses, and yuccas. The burgundy foliage of barberry, smoke bush, and red maple provide strong bolts of color from spring through fall. Textural plants are tucked into crevices between stones, inviting close inspection and exploration.

The September 11, 2001 Remembrance Walkway and Garden honors the Orange County residents and all those who lost their lives on that fateful day. It was dedicated as "A place to honor, reflect, and heal a community and nation." Encircled by a boxwood hedge and flower borders, a rotating black granite globe fountain is surrounded by bronze plaques bearing the names of the 44 Orange County residents who perished that day. A memorial ceremony is held annually on September 11 to honor those who were lost.

The Asian Tea Garden is another lovely area, designed as an Asian stroll garden with a canopy of flowering cherries, gingkos, and Japanese maples. An abstract bluestone walkway leads to a wooden pavilion with a rustic plank table evoking a Japanese teahouse. Large stones provide structure throughout the garden and are softened with plantings of Siberian irises, hydrangeas, Japanese painted ferns, epimediums, and kirengeshomas.

Boscobel House and Gardens

1601 NY-9D, Garrison, NY 10524
845-265-3638
boscobel.org

AREA: 45 acres
HOURS: Grounds: Thurs.–Mon. 9–sunset; house: 11–3, Sat.: 10–3:30. Closed Tues. & Wed.
ADMISSION: Gardens $14; house, gardens & grounds $24
AMENITIES: 🏛️ 👪 🚻
EVENTS: Festivals, tours, talks, concerts, art exhibitions

At the estate's opening celebration in 1961, New York Governor Nelson A. Rockefeller called Boscobel "one of the most beautiful homes ever built in America." A Federal style mansion with unique architectural features, columns, Palladian windows, and ornate exterior decorations, Boscobel had been slated for demolition just six years prior. Originally located 15 miles south in Montrose, the mansion was saved from the wrecking ball by a local grass-roots effort.

After the dramatic rescue, the mansion was dismantled and stored in various barns in the local area until a suitable site could be found. A year later the building was moved in pieces to a beautiful piece of land in Garrison and restoration began.

In 1959 Boscobel's benefactor, Lila Acheson Wallace, brought in the esteemed landscape architecture firm of Innocenti and Webel to create an appropriate historic setting for the newly-restored mansion. Although Boscobel had originally been sited on a working farm, Webel designed a landscape in the Beaux Arts and Neoclassical styles to complement the formal architecture of the house.

Within two years, the garden was completed. To give the feeling that the landscape had always been there, towering maples, weeping cherry trees, mature shrubs and an entire apple orchard were brought in on flatbeds and installed. In the mid-1990s the grounds were expanded to include an additional 29 acres of woodlands—appropriate for an estate whose name comes from Bosco Bello—"pretty woodland." Winding trails lead through woods to an overlook with a rustic gazebo that offers one of the best views of the Hudson River.

Boscobel is a beautiful example of a romantic Beaux Arts garden. A large pond with a tall flume fountain welcomes visitors to the property. Next to the Visitor's Center is a sculpture garden honoring the painters of the 19th-century Hudson River School. A grand allée of maples lines the drive to the forecourt of the mansion. Brick paths lead through the heirloom apple orchard into the formal garden surrounding a classical urn fountain. The Herb Garden around the Orangerie has recently been restored, and features vegetables and herbs that were important for culinary, medicinal, cosmetic and household uses in the 1700s and early 1800s. You will find chamomile, bee balm, rosemary, flax, foxgloves, dill, comfrey, mayapples, lady's mantle, santolina, rue, mints, savory, roses and many other flowers and herbs in raised beds and boxwood parterres. Be sure to walk out to the Belvedere, which offers breathtaking views of the Hudson Highlands, Constitution Marsh, and the West Point Military Academy.

Lasdon Park, Arboretum & Veterans Memorial

2610 Amawalk Rd., Route 35, Katonah, NY 10536
914-864-7263
lasdonpark.org

AREA: 234 acres

HOURS: Park: daily 8–4; museum: weekends 10–3

ADMISSION: Free except special events

AMENITIES: 🍴 👫 🏛 ♿

EVENTS: Gardening Tuesdays, musical events, Holiday Train Show

Located in Westchester County, Lasdon Park is a beautiful property with woodlands, grass meadows, a 20-acre bird and wildlife nature sanctuary, an arboretum of unusual trees, and formal gardens. It was once the country estate of William and Mildred Lasdon who purchased what was then known as Cobbling Rock Farm in 1939. The property featured a three-story Colonial-Revival home modeled after Mount Vernon. William had a strong interest in horticulture and collected many tree specimens during his travels abroad. Upon his death in 1986, the property was sold to Westchester County. Most of the formal gardens remain as they were originally designed by the Lasdons.

The grounds showcase various themed gardens and plant collections. The Lasdon Memorial Garden was established in 2001 by daughter Nan Laitman in honor of her parents. This garden is composed of three separate areas: a fragrance garden of aromatic shrubs and flowers; a synoptic border of shrubs with flowers, berries, and handsome foliage whose botanical genus names begin with letters from A to Z; and a formal garden with seasonal displays of spring tulips, summer annuals, and fall mums encircling a large fountain.

You will find collections of pines, dwarf conifers, azaleas, heathers, magnolias, ornamental trees, and fruit trees throughout the park. A three-acre grove of American chestnut trees is part of a research effort to develop a disease-resistant hybrid for American landscapes. A Historic Tree Walk with QR codes enables you to learn about the species that you encounter. Lasdon Park also features one of the largest collections of lilacs in Westchester County with more than 90 species of lilacs blooming in a profusion of purple, white, and rose in May.

When Jingzhou became a sister city to Westchester County in 1996, a delegation of government officials and businesspeople presented the park with a Chinese pavilion. The beautiful red and teal pavilion was constructed in a traditional process, which took 80 artisans nearly eight months to complete. With its foo dogs, painted dragons, and rooftop animal guardians, the pavilion is the centerpiece of the Chinese Friendship Garden. The surrounding grounds are planted with Asian plants such as willows, ginkgos, Kousa dogwoods, flowering cherries, and bamboo.

For children, the park offers a delightful Dinosaur Garden with statues tucked among the greenery and informational signs that are appropriate for early readers.

Lasdon Park is also home to four memorials and the Westchester County Veterans Museum that exhibits historical documents and memorabilia of Westchester County residents who served in time of war.

Caramoor

149 Girdle Ridge Rd., Katonah, NY 10536
914-232-1252
caramoor.org

AREA: 81 acres

HOURS: Daily 10–4

ADMISSION: Grounds: free; house tour: $15 by appointment

AMENITIES:

EVENTS: Musical performances, Afternoon Teas

Caramoor began as the country estate of the Rosen family in the 1930s. The Rosens were art collectors, musicians, and prominent patrons of music. Today Caramoor is a center for music and art with a Mediterranean mansion surrounded by an Italianate garden.

Walter Tower Rosen was a very successful lawyer, banker, collector, and arts patron, born in Berlin in 1875. His wife, Lucie, came from a socially prominent New York family, was fiercely independent, artistic, and unconventional with interests in fashion, dance, visual arts, and music. After the couple married, they purchased the 100-acre estate in Katonah with its Italianate-style garden. Walter spent ten years designing and building a Tuscan-style villa to hold their collection of art and decorative objects collected from all over the world.

A tour of the Rosen home is a must when visiting the property. The heart of the villa is the Spanish Courtyard, with cloistered walkways enclosing the terrace, flower gardens, and central fountain.

Inside, the house features several complete historic rooms from private villas and chateaux in Italy, France, and England. The Burgundian Library is a French 17th-century paneled room with a brilliant blue vaulted ceiling depicting the stories of Old Testament heroes. The formal dining room features red lacquer furniture, turquoise Chinese export wallpaper with flowering trees and birds, and 17th-century Venetian palace doors. The magnificent music room includes Renaissance furniture and architectural elements such as the intricately carved Italian coffered ceiling, pink marble twisted columns from Verona, Urbino maiolica, and a gorgeous Franco-Flemish tapestry. Here the Rosens hosted friends and neighbors for intimate musical performances, lavish parties, and musical soirées. Their legendary musical evenings were the seeds of today's Summer Music Festival held annually on the estate.

The Caramoor grounds are a blend of historic and contemporary gardens. Greeting you at the main entrance are pollinator gardens planted with phlox, agastache, and coneflowers buzzing with bees and butterflies. The Swiss Pegasus Gate leads into the Sunken Garden, installed by the Rosens' predecessors around 1912. Highly architectural in design, it is enclosed by stucco walls on three sides and features rectangular lawns framed by borders of white hydrangeas and perennials. The elevated Medieval Mount at the rear of the garden features a classical exedra that offers a lovely view of the garden below.

From the Sunken Garden, the 300-foot Cedar Walk leads through the Woodland Garden lined with stands of Eastern and Western arborvitae. Shrouded in climbing hydrangea, the Italian

Pavilion overlooks the Butterfly Garden featuring plants that support all stages of butterfly development. Nearby is the Cutting Garden where flowers are grown for display in the house. Throughout the gardens, you will find interesting architectural details, benches, and fountains. A former dovecote converted into a fountain serves as the centerpiece of the Sense Circle. This area was designed for visitors with visual impairments, with the sound of trickling water and plants that appeal to the senses of touch, taste, and smell.

Lucie Rosen was one of the first performers and a huge patron of the theremin, the world's first electronic instrument. She toured throughout Europe and America advocating for electronic music decades before it became popular. Today, Caramoor hosts an annual Sonic Innovations Exhibition, with contemporary sound-art installations that incorporate natural and human-made sounds with each site's unique acoustic characteristics. The house and grounds are venues for chamber music, jazz, opera, and world music concerts from spring through the holiday season.

Kykuit

381 N. Broadway, Sleepy Hollow, NY (GPS)
914-366-6900
hudsonvalley.org/historic-sites/kykuit

AREA: 249 acres

HOURS: By guided tour only, Mid-May–mid-Nov. See website for days & hours.

ADMISSION: Tours $25 and up

AMENITIES: 🏞 👥 🎟

EVENTS: Various tours offered

The Kykuit estate was home to four generations of the Rockefeller family and features a grand mansion, beautiful gardens, extraordinary art, and spectacular scenery. It has been meticulously maintained for more than 100 years, and is a site of the National Trust for Historic Preservation. Kykuit is accessible by formal tours only. There are four to choose from, ranging from 1.5 to 3 hours in length, depending on how much you would like to see of the mansion; the Coach Barn, with its collections of classic automobiles and horse-drawn carriages; and the gardens. Only the Landmark Tour and Grand Tour offer access to all of the gardens.

Kykuit, Dutch for "lookout" and pronounced "kei-kit", is situated on the highest point in the hamlet of Pocantico Hills, overlooking the Hudson River at Tappan Zee. It has a view of the New York

City skyline, 25 miles to the south. The imposing mansion, built of local stone and topped with the Rockefeller emblem, is located centrally in a 249-acre gated inner compound within the larger Rockefeller family estate.

The 40-room mansion was built in 1908 by John D. Rockefeller, founder of Standard Oil, and the richest man in America in his day. The initial plans for the property were developed by the company of Frederick Law Olmsted. Rockefeller was unhappy with their work, however, and assumed control of the design himself. He created several scenic winding roads and lookouts and transplanted mature trees to realize his vision.

In 1906, the oversight of the house and grounds was given to son John, who hired landscape architect William Welles Bosworth. Kykuit is considered Bosworth's best work in the United States. The design is loosely based on traditional Italian gardens, with strong axes, terraces, fountains, pavilions, and classical ornamentation. The terraced gardens include a Morning Garden, Grand Staircase, Japanese Garden, Italian Garden, Japanese-style brook, Japanese Teahouse, loggia, Temple of Aphrodite, and a semicircular rose garden. With stairways leading you from one level to the next, the garden invites movement and views.

The Rockefellers planned to use the house only in spring and fall, so trees were selected for their spring bloom, such as cherries and dogwoods, or for their autumn leaf color, such as the Japanese maples. Wisteria is one of the prevailing plants that ties the garden together—you first see it on the front façade of the house, and then it reappears on walls and pergolas throughout the garden. Fountains are another signature element, from the replica of a Boboli Gardens fountain with a 30-foot statue of Oceanus that greets you in the forecourt, to 39 other fountains that punctuate the garden rooms. The inner garden has a Moorish

theme, with a canal and a small fountain featuring a sculpted fountainhead and bronze swans. The gardens, which took over seven years to install, were completed in 1915, and exceeded their budget of $30,000 by one million dollars.

Governor Nelson Rockefeller, the last private owner of Kykuit, transformed its basement passages into a major private art gallery containing paintings by Picasso, Chagall, and Warhol, as well as extraordinary Picasso tapestries. Between 1935 and the late 1970s Governor Rockefeller added more than 120 works of abstract and modern sculpture to the gardens, including works by Picasso, Brancusi, Appel, Arp, Calder, Moore, and Giacometti. He precisely and skillfully sited the art to complement the classical formality of the garden and create stunning views. Their inclusion in the garden elevated it from a beautiful classic garden to an extraordinary experience of architecture, horticulture, and art.

Lyndhurst

635 S. Broadway, Tarrytown, NY 10591
914-631-4481
lyndhurst.org

AREA: 67 acres

HOURS: Grounds: April–Dec.: daily 9:30–4:30; house: by tour only: April-Dec.

ADMISSION: Grounds: $10; house tours: $25 and up

AMENITIES: 🏛️ 🚻 🏪

EVENTS: Landscape tours, concerts, holiday weekend

Overlooking the Hudson River in Tarrytown, Lyndhurst is one of America's finest Gothic Revival mansions with a rich history spanning over 200 years. It also has one of the most significant and well-documented landscapes that illustrates two centuries of changing landscape fashions in the United States.

Lyndhurst was built as a summer home in 1942 for William Paulding Jr., a former brigadier general and mayor of New York City. Architect Alexander Jackson Davis designed the mansion in a romantic Gothic Revival style, with picturesque-style grounds of sweeping vistas, winding carriage roads, and artfully positioned trees.

In the 1860s, second owner George Merritt commissioned Davis to double the size of the mansion and converted it into a full-time residence worthy of a wealthy merchant. He hired Bavarian landscape gardener Ferdinand Mangold to incorporate the latest landscape trends from European royal estates at Lyndhurst. Merritt and Mangold developed an elegant parkland around the mansion with specimen trees and walkways offering views of the river. Merritt renamed the estate "Lyndhurst" after the large linden trees that he had planted. He also commissioned Lord & Burnham to build the largest private greenhouse, which was designed in a grand Moorish style.

Railroad tycoon and financier Jay Gould purchased the estate in 1880 as a family summer home and an escape from the pressures of business life in the city. Gould had a strong affection for nature and flowers and made few changes to the house. Instead, he built a 380-foot-long greenhouse after the original burned to the ground. The new greenhouse housed more than 40,000 varieties of plants from all over the globe, including thousands of orchids. In the late 1800s, wealthy Europeans and Americans got caught up in a craze for orchids that became known as "orchidelirium." Collectors traveled the world in a race to acquire the rarest orchids for their collections.

Gould's eldest daughter, Helen, became the steward of Lyndhurst after her father's death in 1892. Helen was an educated woman and a well-loved philanthropist. During her stewardship, the estate became the site of free sewing, cooking, and carpentry schools for disadvantaged children so they could break the cycle of poverty. The massive greenhouse and pool building were open to the community six days a week. Like her father, Helen was an avid gardener and naturalist and made sure that all of the children at Lyndhurst spent time planting and gardening. Helen added the rose garden in 1914. Planted in a concentric circle design, the garden contained 500 roses, with the oldest varieties in the outer beds.

Helen's sister Anna married into the French aristocracy and lived most of her adult life in France. After Helen's death in 1938, Anna used Lyndhurst for charitable efforts such as a convalescent home for soldiers and seamen. She auctioned off the contents of the greenhouse to benefit the American Red Cross. When she passed away in 1961, she bequeathed the entire estate to the National Trust for Historic Preservation.

Today, the landscape is in the midst of a 10-year restoration that began in 2020. Plans include the restoration of the historic rockeries, kitchen garden, fruit orchard, rose garden, and perennial gardens as well as allées of flowering trees. The massive treehouse will be rebuilt, and the historic greenhouse will be restored to its former glory.

Untermyer Gardens

945 N. Broadway, Yonkers, NY 10701
914-613-4502
untermyergardens.org

AREA: 43 acres

HOURS: May 1–Aug. 31: daily 7–7. See website for other hours.

ADMISSION: Free

AMENITIES:

EVENTS: Various tours, winter lectures, symposia, holiday illuminations

When Samuel Untermyer purchased Greystone Mansion in 1899, he set out to build "the finest garden in the world." Untermyer was a highly successful lawyer and businessman who was instrumental in the establishment of the Federal Reserve System. He was also passionately interested in and knowledgeable about horticulture. After purchasing Greystone, he acquired neighboring properties to expand his grounds to more than 150 acres. In 1916 Untermyer hired Beaux Arts architect William Welles Bosworth to design the gardens. Bosworth drew inspiration from the great gardens and architecture of Persia, India, Pakistan, Spain, and Italy to create a unique garden that evokes multiple ancient cultures.

In the 41 years that Untermyer owned Greystone, he transformed the estate into one of the finest gardens in America. Supplied by 60 greenhouses and maintained by 60 gardeners, the gardens were a great source of pride for Untermyer. Wanting to share his paradise with the public, he opened the gardens once a week during the 1920s and 1930s. Untermyer wanted the property to become a public park after his death, but the gardens were too costly for the county or state to maintain. Ultimately, a 43-acre core part of the property was given to the City of Yonkers, and the Untermyer Garden Conservancy was founded in 2011 to restore the gardens to their former splendor.

The centerpiece of the property is the Walled Garden, based on the Garden of Eden in the book of Genesis. Entered by a grand Mycenaean gate, the garden is the finest example of an Indo-Persian garden in America. The main axis is created by four canals that symbolize the four rivers of Paradise, while the four garden quadrants represent the elements of earth, fire, air, and water. The canals are lined with flower beds punctuated by Japanese hollies. In the spring they feature a great display of tulips, followed by colorful annuals and dramatic tropicals in the summer. These displays change from year to year as they would have in Untermyer's time.

The main axis leads to a large pool with water lilies and an amphitheater flanked by two sphinxes set on marble columns. To the west, the Greek-inspired Temple of the Sky overlooks a Persian pool in the lower terrace. Corinthian columns encircle a mosaic floor based on a 900-year-old Mycenean wall fresco depicting spirals and lotus blossoms. The crenellated walls of the garden are lined with mixed beds of perennials, shrubs, vines, and trees.

A doorway in the Walled Garden leads to the Vista, a magnificent staircase leading down to the Hudson River. The stairs are lined with a dramatic combination of Japanese cedars and variegated Hakone grass. At the bottom of the Vista is the Overlook, a platform with two ancient Roman monolithic marble columns that frame a magnificent view of the river and the Palisades. Adjacent to the Vista, the former Rose and Dahlia Gardens were transformed into a formal vegetable garden and orchard in 2023.

Another stunning feature of the property is the Temple of Love, a round summerhouse crowning the elaborate rock garden. While the temple offers glorious views of the river and the Palisades, the rock garden is best seen from below with waterfalls cascading to the rocky pool. A rough-hewn staircase allows you to climb up through the grotto into the temple above. The rock and stream gardens are elaborately planted with pollinator plants, ornamental grasses, and dwarf conifers.

The Met Cloisters

99 Margaret Corbin Dr., Fort Tryon Park, New York, NY 10040
212-923-3700
metmuseum.org/visit/plan-your-visit/met-cloisters

AREA: 1 acre
HOURS: Thurs.–Tues.: 10–4:30
ADMISSION: $30
AMENITIES:
EVENTS: Various cultural and family events

A branch of The Metropolitan Museum of Art, The Cloisters is the only museum dedicated to the art of the Middle Ages in the United States. Incorporating five medieval cloisters, the museum evokes the architecture of the Middle Ages and displays medieval metalwork, painting, sculpture, stained glass, and textiles. It is also renowned for its three cloister gardens, which were designed as an integral part of the museum when it was built in 1938.

The Romanesque Cuxa Cloister was originally part of a 12th-century Benedictine monastery in the northeast Pyrenees. Its columns and octagonal fountain are carved from a mottled pink-and-white marble found in Languedoc. The Judy Black Garden within this cloister is divided into quadrants by crossed paths. Each quadrant features a grass plot with a pollarded apple tree bordered

by ornamental flowers and herbs that add beauty and fragrance. Medieval plants are supplemented with modern varieties to provide a long season of bloom, beginning with early crocuses and snow-drops, followed by columbines, pinks, bellflowers, foxgloves, daisies, poppies, and many other flow-ers that bloom until late fall. In winter the arcades are glassed in, and the interior walkways are filled with pots of citrus, jasmine, rosemary, and bay.

The Gothic Bonnefont Cloister comes from a Cistercian abbey in southwest France and dates back to 1300. This is a medieval herb garden with garden beds arranged symmetrically around a 15th-century Venetian wellhead. It features more than 400 species of plants and herbs used in the Middle Ages. Some were grown in gardens while others were collected from the wild or imported in dried form. Plants are grown in raised beds enclosed with wattle fences and grouped accord-ing to their medieval use: cooking, medicine, art, industry, housekeeping, love, fertility, and magic. Tender plants such as turmeric, ginger, frankin-cense, and cardamom are grown in terra-cotta pots that can be moved inside in winter. Adjacent to the Bonnefont Garden is an orchard of lady apples and other medieval fruits such as medlar, quince, currants, and elderberries. The trees are underplanted with a meadow of spring bulbs and colorful summer flowers and herbs.

The Gothic Trie Cloister is from the Trie-en-Bigorre region of southwest France. It dates to the late 15th century, and its exuberant carvings portray biblical scenes and saints' legends as well as grotesques and coats of arms. Of The Cloister's three gardens, this one is the most informal. It is a colorful fantasy garden of flowers and fruits based on the Unicorn Tapestries. It features more than 50 species of plants found in the famous tapestries, including many varieties of pinks, violets, prim-roses, bellflowers, and wild strawberries.

Heather Garden

Center Path, Fort Tryon Park, New York, NY 10040
212-795-1388
forttryonparktrust.org

AREA: 3 acre garden
HOURS: Daily 6 am–1 am
ADMISSION: Free
AMENITIES:
EVENTS: Spring Community Parade, Urban Wildlife Festival, many cultural and family events

The three-acre Heather Garden is the crown jewel of Fort Tryon Park with a stunning 600-foot perennial border punctuated with heaths and heathers as well as other flowering trees and shrubs. It began as the vision of John D. Rockefeller, Jr. who collaborated with the Olmsted Brothers to create a picturesque park overlooking the Hudson River.

During the 19th and early 20th centuries, Fort Tryon was home to several beautiful estates. Rockefeller began acquiring these estates as they came up for sale, gradually assembling 67 acres that he gave to the city for a public park. Rockefeller hired the illustrious Olmsted Brothers firm to design Fort Tryon Park in their signature picturesque landscape style that would preserve the spectacular vistas of the Hudson River and the Palisades. The site provided many challenges with its steep, rocky topography and thin soil. It

took four years to transform it into a manicured landscape with promenades, stone retaining walls, terraced wooded slopes, lush gardens, and eight miles of paths for pedestrians.

The Heather Garden was to be a distinct area of beauty within the park, built into the side of a rocky ridge. Low-growing heather was chosen as the predominant plant so it would not obscure the views. Since its completion in 1935, the park has been restored several times. The latest renovation of the Heather Garden was completed in 2010 by landscape designers Lynden B. Miller and Ronda M. Brands. The result is a spectacular flower garden with 550 varieties of plants. The garden is bisected by a central path. On one side is the perennial border with old-world roses, historic azaleas, hydrangeas, and other flowering shrubs that provide year-round structure for the ever-changing tapestry of perennials. On the other side of the path is the heather bed, anchored by several historic yews and a massive Siberian elm. More than 30 varieties of heaths and heathers hark back to the garden's original design. They are set amidst companion plantings of perennials, conifers, and ornamental trees. The topography and plantings vary from rocky slopes hosting delicate alpines to meadow-style plantings of sun-loving flowers.

In the spring, flowering dogwoods, rhododendrons, and azaleas complement peonies, candytuft, irises, poppies, and salvias. Summer brings on yarrows, globe thistles, roses, catmint, and astilbes. Butterfly weeds, red hot pokers, black-eyed Susans, and coneflowers provide food for pollinators. In the fall, dramatic color arrives with spectacular fall foliage and the blooms of asters, anemones, stonecrops, and hydrangeas. Throughout the seasons, foliage plants like purple smoke bush and heuchera provide long-lasting pops of color while clematis, hyacinth bean, and other vines trained on teepees add vertical interest.

Wave Hill

4900 Independence Ave., Bronx, NY 10471
718-549-3200
wavehill.org

AREA: 28 acres

HOURS: Tues.–Sun. 10–4:30

ADMISSION: $10, parking fee

AMENITIES: 🅰️ 🅱️ 🅲️ ❌

EVENTS: Public Garden & Conservatory walks, educational and children's programs

Wave Hill has been a public garden since 1965, but it began as an estate built by William Lewis Morris in 1844. Later, it was the home of New York publisher William Henry Appleton and attracted such famous figures as Theodore Roosevelt and Mark Twain. It was the final owner, George W. Perkins, who created an esteemed garden and left the property to the public.

Perkins was a wealthy financier and partner of J. P. Morgan. He retired at the age of 50 to devote himself to public causes. He was particularly interested in conservation and masterminded the creation of the 700-acre Palisades Park. Perkins purchased Wave Hill in 1893 and gradually added surrounding properties to assemble an 80-acre estate. He was keenly interested in horticulture and landscape design, and he unified the separate estates with naturalistic paths, fieldstone walls, and ornamental plantings. To house his collections of rare

plants and to enjoy fresh produce year-round, he built the Palm House and adjoining greenhouses that formed the centerpiece of the garden. He also built a large, three-story underground recreation building covered by a landscaped terrace crowned with an Italianate pergola.

Today, Wave Hill is a collection of innovative gardens that reflect the creative spirit of the horticultural staff. This spirit of experimentation was fostered by Marco Polo Stufano, Wave Hill's founding director of horticulture, who set the tone for more than 30 years. Situated on the Great Lawn, the Pergola frames the majestic views of the Hudson River and the Palisades beyond. It supports a large hardy kiwi vine that forms a green roof. This shady respite is ideal for visitors as well as the shade-loving tropical plants that enhance this area during the warmer months. Adjacent to the Pergola is the Arts and Crafts-inspired Flower Garden. Enclosed by a rustic cedar fence shrouded in clematis 'Rubromarginata,' it displays an informal tapestry of bulbs, heirloom and modern perennials, annuals, shrubs, and tender exotics that bloom in lavish succession. Nearby you will also find the splashy Paisley Bed, a nod to seasonal bedding that was very popular during the Victorian era. The spring display of flowering bulbs is followed by a warm-season planting of colorful annuals, tropicals, or cacti and succulents, which change from year to year.

The historic conservatory is home to plants from warmer regions of the world: palms, ferns, bromeliads, orchids, cacti, and succulents. Behind the conservatory are the terraced Herb and Dry gardens, built on the stone foundations of the estate's vegetable and flower glasshouses. The sheltering walls and sunny aspect create a warm microclimate for the plants here. The Herb Garden is a teaching garden, with 88 beds bursting with culinary, medicinal, and dye herbs. The Dry

Garden features Mediterranean ornamentals that thrive in well-drained soil and warm, dry climates. Overlooking these gardens is the alpine house and terrace, with diminutive rock garden plants grown in handmade hypertufa troughs.

Another interesting area is the Wild Garden, based on the concept of a "managed wilderness" championed by Irish designer William Robinson in the 1870s. Winding paths lead through a naturalistic hillside bursting with plants that appear self-sown but are actually a highly curated collection. Located at the highest point in the property, this garden offers beautiful views and benches that invite you to linger.

Situated just north of the Wild Garden, the formal Aquatic and Monocot gardens provide a sharp contrast in style and plant selection. An ornamental pool flanked by symmetrical stone pergolas and trimmed hedges creates a strong architectural statement. The pool is home to both tropical and hardy water lilies and other aquatic plants. The nearby garden features a collection of monocotyledons—plants whose seeds contain one single leaf, including ornamental grasses, elephant ears, cannas, bananas, gingers, and others. The surrounding grounds are graced with some of the oldest and largest tree specimens of European beech, oak, dawn redwood, American elm, lacebark pine, and Japanese maple in the area.

New York Botanical Garden

2900 Southern Blvd., Bronx, NY 10458
718-817-8700
nybg.org

AREA: 250 acres

HOURS: Tues.–Sun. 10–6; open holiday Mondays

ADMISSION: $23 weekdays, $28 weekends

AMENITIES:

EVENTS: Orchid Show, Daffodil Weekend, Plant Sale, Mother's Day Garden Party & much more

The New York Botanical Garden (NYBG) is a 250-acre living museum that showcases more than a million plants in extensive collections. It's also an educational center, open-air classroom, urban park, major arboretum, collection of display gardens, and a renowned research facility. It operates one of the world's largest plant-research and conservation programs, with nearly 200 staff members—including 80 Ph.D. scientists—working in its state-of-the-art molecular labs as well as in the field.

NYBG was founded by Nathaniel Lord Britton and his wife, Elizabeth—the 19th century's "power botany couple." He was a professor of botany and geology at Columbia University and an expert on plants of the Caribbean. She was one of the few women scientists of her time, and a leading scholar of mosses and wildflowers. The couple visited Britain's Kew Gardens during their honeymoon in 1888, and proposed a botanic garden for their native state of New York shortly after. Nathaniel was the first director, a position he held for more than 30 years.

The Bronx site was selected for the botanical garden due to the beauty and diversity of its natural landscape. Notable architects and landscape designers collaborated to create the garden as it is today. Calvert Vaux designed the overall layout of the grounds, including the buildings and the elegant carriage routes that wind around rock outcrops, hills, dales, and forests. The Olmsted brothers formalized the master plan in the 1920s. Beatrix Farrand designed the rose garden. Marian Cruger Coffin laid out the ornamental conifer and lilac collections. Ellen Biddle Shipman created a long perennial border called the Ladies' Border. And T.H. Everett created the rock garden.

You can visit any month of the year—just make sure that you allow a whole day! NYBG has some of the largest plant collections in the world, including ones devoted to daffodils, azaleas, cherries, crabapples, magnolias, tree peonies, herbaceous peonies, conifers, daylilies, and lotus.

The display gardens provide interest in all seasons. The 2.5-acre Rock Garden is an oasis of jewel-like alpine flowers nestled among its gravel beds, rocks, and crevices. A gently cascading waterfall and stream flow to a tranquil pond. In May the surrounding native dogwoods bloom with breathtaking swaths of tiarella, trilliums, and other spring wildflowers.

The Perennial Garden is stunning in spring with hundreds of tulips interplanted among bleeding hearts and other early perennials. Its four themed rooms contain distinctive collections of plants selected for their color or seasonality. Peak time is in summer when countless brilliant flowers bloom in waves of purple, pink, yellow, and red.

Penelope Hobhouse designed the Herb Garden. The evergreen boxwood parterre framework provides symmetry and structure for the soft beauty and fragrance of the herbs.

The Peggy Rockefeller Rose Garden is considered to be among the world's best rose collections. The triangular shaped garden was completed in 1988 and features more than 650 varieties of roses around a central gazebo.

The Lord & Burnham Conservatory is a remarkable example of Victorian-style glasshouse artistry. It is home to lush tropical rain forests, cactus-filled deserts, orchids, palms, aquatic and carnivorous plants, and seasonal displays. Of special note is the annual Orchid Show designed with a different theme each year, featuring thousands of gorgeous orchids.

NEW JERSEY
Suggested Daily Itineraries

Van Vleck House & Gardens,
Montclair (3)
Lunch–DeNovo European Pub, Montclair
Avis Campbell Gardens, Montclair (5)
Presby Memorial Iris Gardens,
Montclair (4)

Greenwood Gardens, Short Hills (7)
Lunch–The Huntley Taverne, Summit
Reeves-Reed Arboretum, Summit (8)

Frelinghuysen Arboretum,
Morristown (6)
Lunch–Sette, Bernardsville
Cross Estate Gardens, Bernardsville (11)
Peony's Envy, Bernardsville (12)

Laurelwood Arboretum, Wayne (2)
Lunch–Vila Verde, Wayne
New Jersey Botanical Garden,
Ringwood (1)

Bamboo Brook Outdoor Education
Center, Far Hills (14)
Willowwood Arboretum, Far Hills (13)
Lunch–Gladstone Tavern, Gladstone
Leonard J. Buck Garden, Far Hills (15)

Sayen House & Gardens, Hamilton
Square (20)
Lunch–Grounds for Sculpture, Hamilton
Grounds for Sculpture, Hamilton (21)

Prospect House, Princeton (18)
Lunch–Agricola, Princeton
Morven Museum & Gardens,
Princeton (17)

NEW JERSEY

New Jersey Botanical Garden

Morris Rd., Ringwood, NJ 07456
973-962-9534
njbg.org

AREA: 96 acres

HOURS: Daily 8–8

ADMISSION: Free

AMENITIES: 👥 👥

EVENTS: Plant sale in May, garden tours, manor tours, concerts, festivals, wildflower and tree walks

The New Jersey Botanical Garden is part of Skylands, a historic estate in the Ramapo Mountains. Originally established by New York City lawyer Francis Lynde Stetson, the estate was sold to investment banker Clarence McKenzie Lewis in 1922. Both men were trustees of the New York Botanical Garden, and the property benefited from their care. Lewis transformed Skylands into a horticultural showplace. He removed Stetson's house and replaced it with a 45-room Tudor Manor House designed by John Russell Pope. The granite was quarried from the property, and many of the rooms contain antique paneling and stained glass, some of which date back to the 16th century.

To create Skylands' country-estate landscape, Lewis hired the prominent firm of Vitale and Geiffert, and was actively involved in the project, stressing symmetry, color, texture, and fragrance in the gardens. He spent 30 years gathering plants locally and abroad and amassed one of the finest plant collections in New Jersey. In peak seasons he employed more than 60 gardeners.

In 1966 the State of New Jersey purchased the entire property, and the 96 acres surrounding the manor were designated as the state's official botanical garden. The elegantly landscaped grounds showcase more than 5,000 species of trees, shrubs, and flowers, and the specialty gardens provide something to see in all seasons. The east side of the manor house overlooks a series of five distinctive terraces. The first features the Octagonal Garden—an elevated rock garden with miniature alpine plants surrounding an octagonal pool. The second terrace is a fragrance garden, with a Magnolia Walk of sweetbay magnolias, viburnums, honeysuckles, and mahonias. This collection was situated near the house so that the scents would drift through the windows in June. In the third level's Azalea Garden, rhododendrons and double-flowering dogwoods surround a reflecting pool with a grotto, koi, and water lilies. Daylilies and annuals bloom in the fourth terrace's Summer Garden. And the fifth culminates in the Peony Garden with its Memory Bench; there, tree peonies bloom in May. Flanking the terrace gardens are the Pinetum and the Lilac Garden, which contains more than 100 lilac varieties, including French hybrids, Japanese tree lilacs, and Chinese lilacs that peak in mid-May.

On the west side of the manor, the Winter Garden displays colorful evergreens and stately trees, including a magnificent copper beech, a Japanese umbrella pine, an Algerian fir, an Atlas cedar indigenous to North Africa, and the red oak that has stood in front of the library since the 1890s.

Crossing the road you will find yourself in the Annual Garden, which is anchored by a 16th century

Italian marble wellhead, and the Perennial Garden, now restored to Lewis' original design. The Crab Apple Vista, an allée of 166 trees stretching a half mile, is a triumph of pink blossoms in early May. The Wildflower Garden features a beautiful display of Japanese primroses around its Bog Pond. Hosta collectors will appreciate the fenced Hosta/Rhododendron Garden. The most unlikely of gardening sites is the Moraine Garden planted in the rock deposit left by Ice Age glaciers. Heathers, sedums, dwarf conifers, and ground-hugging alpines thrive in this ancient spot.

Laurelwood Arboretum

725 Pines Lake Drive West, Wayne, NJ 07470
973-831-5675
laurelwoodarboretum.org

AREA: 30 acres

HOURS: Daily 8 am–dusk; visitor center: April–Oct.: Tues.–Sun. 12–4

ADMISSION: Free, donations welcome

AMENITIES: 👥

EVENTS: Cell phone tours, plant sale, lectures

Laurelwood Arboretum is a botanical park offering woodland paths, ponds, streams, and gardens with a special focus on rhododendrons and azaleas. With a sculpture trail, it is an ideal destination for nature lovers, artists, and photographers.

The 30-acre property was purchased in the 1940s by Pine Lake residents Dorothy and John Knippenberg. They founded a commercial nursery on the site called Laurelwood Gardens that specialized in rhododendrons and azaleas. Dorothy was a keen horticulturist and began hybridizing rhododendrons and azaleas in 1955. Her goal was to develop hardy large-leaved varieties with massive flower trusses and late bloom. She was very involved in the international hybridizing community and donated cuttings, seeds, and pollen to growers all over the world. The new cultivars,

often numbering in the thousands, were raised, grown, and evaluated on a hillside test garden. Eight of her named hybrids were registered, including the locally named 'Laurel Pink,' 'Laurelwood Snow Bunting,' and 'Wayne Pink.'

The Knippenbergs donated Laurelwood to Wayne Township in the 1960s to be used as a public park. Their rhododendron and azalea collections form the backbone of this garden, augmented by specimen trees and shrubs as well as themed gardens. Blooms can be enjoyed from spring through fall, beginning with witch hazels, hellebores, magnolias, early bulbs, and daffodils. The heady fragrance of lilacs along the Lilac Walk scents the garden in late April. Azalea Way is spectacular in mid-May when hybrid azaleas bred by Joseph Gable explode in shades of pink, white, red, and orange. Hundreds of rhododendrons bloom from mid-May to June, many of them hybridized by the Knippenbergs and early pioneers such as Charles O. Dexter, Guy Nearing, and David Gable. The Pollinator Garden is most colorful in midsummer when coneflowers, phloxes, bee balms, liatrises, and milkweeds attract bees, moths, butterflies, and hummingbirds. Asters, beautyberries, hollies, and the brilliant foliage of deciduous trees create a vibrant display in autumn.

Van Vleck House & Gardens

21 Van Vleck St., Montclair, NJ 07042
973-744-4752
montclairfoundation.org

AREA: 6 acres

HOURS: Daily dawn–dusk

ADMISSION: Free

AMENITIES:

EVENTS: Guided walks, lectures, workshops

Van Vleck House & Gardens provides an excellent example of the large homes built in this New York City suburb during the late 1800s. Three generations of the Van Vleck family lived on the six-acre property and designed the imposing and elegant dwellings and gardens.

Shortly after the railroad reached Montclair in the mid-1800s, mining and lumber executive Joseph Van Vleck moved his wife and 10 children from Brooklyn to this quiet suburb, where he built a family compound. The elegant Mediterranean-style villa that now graces the grounds was designed and built in 1916 by his son Joseph Jr., who also created an Italianate green garden around the house. In 1939 Joseph Jr.'s son, Howard, took up residence in the villa with his wife and four children. Like his father, Howard pursued a career in architecture and had a passion for the arts and horticulture. He left the professional field in 1930 to pursue his interests in painting and gardening full time, and redesigned the gardens to be more colorful and family-friendly. He enjoyed

hybridizing rhododendrons and strove to create a clear, yellow-flowering variety. A number of his hybrids survive as sentimental specimens in the garden, and several have been registered and named in memory of Van Vleck family members.

In 1993, Howard's heirs donated the property to The Montclair Foundation. This community foundation transformed the house into a center for nonprofits, and opened the garden to the public. A cell phone tour serves as a guide to the landscape. The most impressive feature of the garden is the enormous Chinese wisteria, planted in 1929. Although a vine, it has a trunk the girth of a mature tree. Circling the house's courtyard and winding up to the mansion's second floor, the wisteria is in its glory in mid-May.

The garden is sheltered from surrounding streets with plantings of mature conifers and broad-leaved evergreens that are also used to create separate garden rooms within. There are stunning collections of rhododendrons and azaleas, many of which Howard grew from cuttings. Formal lawns are bordered by long pergolas and walkways designed for strolling. Intimate garden nooks are furnished with benches. A second wisteria-covered pergola overlooks the site of a former tennis court, which has been transformed into a classical garden with an urn fountain. The Formal Garden behind the house features beautifully planted perennial beds. The best time to view the original plantings is in May, when the rhododendrons, azaleas, and magnolias are in full bloom, but the garden offers horticultural interest year-round.

At the back of the property, a former garage and the gardener's quarters with its adjoining greenhouse reference the separate houses they once served. Both were designed by Joseph Jr., and now serve as the Education and Visitor Center.

Presby Memorial Iris Gardens

474 Upper Mountain Ave., Montclair, NJ 07043
973-783-5974
presbyirisgardens.org

AREA: 8 acres

HOURS: Daily dawn–dusk

ADMISSION: Suggested donation $8

AMENITIES:

EVENTS: Plant sale Mother's Day weekend and following May weekends

Cultivated in New England since early colonial times, irises have a long and revered history. The Greek goddess Iris was the messenger of the gods and the personification of the rainbow. The fleur-de-lis is derived from the shape of the iris and is the symbol of the royal family of France. In Japan, the rhizome was ground to create the white face makeup for the geisha. And in New Jersey, irises are the stars of this memorial garden.

Frank H. Presby (1857–1924) was a leading citizen of Montclair and an iris hybridizer, collector, and founder of the American Iris Society. It was his expressed wish to give a collection of his favorite flower to Montclair's newly acquired Mountainside Park. However, he passed away in 1924 before he could carry out his plan. The Presby Gardens were established thanks to local resident Barbara

Walther, who led the effort and watched over the garden for 50 years.

Located at the base of the 7.5-acre park, the gardens were designed in 1927 by John C. Wister, a Harvard University landscape architect. He designed the garden in a bow shape, and Presby Gardens is now referred to as the "rainbow on the hill." The iris garden contains more than 10,000 irises of approximately 1,500 varieties, which produce more than 100,000 blooms over the course of the season. Peak bloom time is mid-May through the first week of June. Many of these irises were donated from Presby's and Wister's personal gardens, as well as from private Montclair gardens, the American Iris Society, and hybridizers all over the world.

Every iris in the garden has a marker indicating the name of the iris, the hybridizer, and the year the iris was registered with the American Iris Society. Twenty-six beds contain bearded irises, each dedicated to a particular decade. Be sure to look for the Heirloom Iris beds (beds 5a & 5b) with plants dating from the 16th to the 20th centuries. Also look for the dwarf irises, growing only to 8 inches in height. They are the earliest of the bearded iris to bloom, and are ideal for rock gardens and fronts of borders.

Beds running along the creek bed contain a collection of non-bearded Spuria, Siberian, Japanese, and Louisiana irises, which prefer a wetter setting. Purple weeping beeches, fringe trees, katsuras, stewartias, redbuds, and ginkgos provide an interesting border for the iris gardens. A bee sanctuary with seven hives was added in 2000.

Avis Campbell Gardens

60 S. Fullerton Ave., Montclair, NJ 07042
gardenclubofmontclair.com/avis-campbell-gardens

AREA: .3 acres

HOURS: Daily dawn–dusk

ADMISSION: Free

EVENTS: Educational events

Avis Campbell Gardens is truly a secret garden that is tucked behind 60 South Fullerton Avenue adjacent to the Montclair Library. It is the pride and joy of the Garden Club of Montclair whose members have been caring for this hidden gem for over 70 years.

Founded in 1926, the Garden Club of Montclair had to limit its membership until a suitably large meeting space became available. In 1952 the club moved into the Davela Mills Building, which featured an empty lot perfect for a garden. Montclair

landscape architect Avis Campbell designed a "Wheel of Life" garden around a central octagonal pool with a fountain. The paths forming the spokes of the wheel divided the garden into individual garden beds that could have their own planting schemes. Installation of the garden involved the whole community. Local scout troops and garden club members cleared the site, laid the brick paths, prepared the soil, and planted 1,500 tulip bulbs donated by a local business as well as all of the flowers. Jackson & Perkins donated 195 roses. Since then, garden club members gather every Tuesday morning from early spring through late fall to plant, weed, prune, and feed the garden.

A long brick wall swathed in 'New Dawn' and 'Sombreil' roses, ivy, and climbing hydrangeas encloses one side of the garden, creating the feeling of a secluded courtyard. An arched entryway frames your view of the garden's central axis and its beautiful fountain. In the spring you will find the garden bursting with colorful tulips. These give way to heirloom peonies, Siberian irises, baptisias, daisies, lupines, salvias, foxgloves, lady's mantles, and dozens of other perennials. Six of the beds are planted with 127 hybrid tea and floribunda roses that bloom from June until October. Lamb's ears, sedums, Japanese forest grass, spireas, and weigelas contribute long-lasting color with their silver, gold, and maroon foliage.

The 9/11 Memorial Bed offers a spot for peaceful reflection with a tranquil color palette of white, blue, and green. Shaded by two Japanese snowbell trees with their delicate white blossoms, the bed is simply planted with evergreen vinca and seasonal white tulips, geraniums, and mums.

Frelinghuysen Arboretum

353 E. Hanover Ave., Morristown, NJ 07960
973-326-7603
morrisparks.net

AREA: 127 acres

HOURS: Grounds daily 8 am–sunset; Visitor Center: Thurs.–Sun. 10–4

ADMISSION: Free

AMENITIES: 👥 🍽️

EVENTS: Plant sale, flower shows, programs & events

The Frelinghuysen Arboretum began as Whippany Farm, and was the country home of patent attorney George Griswold Frelinghuysen and his wife, Sara Ballantine Frelinghuysen, whose grandfather founded the Ballantine Brewing Company. The Frelinghuysens commissioned Boston architectural firm Rotch & Tilden to construct a summer home and carriage house on the property. The mansion, a fine example of Colonial Revival architecture, was built in 1891 and fashioned with Federal urns and swags, ionic columns on the porte cochere, and a large Palladian window on the second-floor landing.

The Frelinghuysens spent 40 summers at Whippany Farm and their winters in New York City. Their summer home was a working farm with greenhouses, barns, and outbuildings, and produced vegetables and flowers which were sent to the family in New York City via train.

Scottish landscape architect James McPherson designed the grounds in the style of an English country estate, with large trees, a Great Lawn, gazebo, knot garden, rock labyrinth, and a perennial and fountain garden. In 1920 Sara planted the formal Rose Garden, with beds laid out between the spokes of a Chippendale-style brick walkway set in a basket weave pattern.

The Frelinghuysens' daughter, Matilda, bequeathed the farm to Morris County in 1969. It was dedicated as the Frelinghuysen Arboretum in 1971 and put on the National Register of Historic Places in 1977. The formal gardens around the house were restored with plantings of spring tulips and summer annuals. Trees in the park include willow, magnolia, bald cypress, beeches, crabapples, and flowering cherries. The park commission has added a series of educational demonstration gardens, such as color-themed gardens, shade and fern gardens, rock gardens, and raised gardens for visitors with special needs.

Greenwood Gardens

274 Old Short Hills Rd., Short Hills, NJ 07078
973-258-4026
greenwoodgardens.org

AREA: 28 acres
HOURS: May–early Nov.: Fri.–Sun. 10–5, select holidays
ADMISSION: $15
AMENITIES:
EVENTS: Bird walks, plant walks, twilight tours & more

Two very different American families left their marks on Greenwood Gardens. In the early 1900s, Joseph P. Day, a real estate auctioneer and self-made multi-millionaire, built the mansion and gardens as a retreat from hectic city life. Architect William Whetten Renwick designed both home and garden in an exuberant, heavily ornamented style. The garden was influenced by both Italian and Arts and Crafts styles, and laid out with strict axes and vistas. A series of lavishly planted terraces descended from the house, and an extensive system of paths made from exposed aggregate pavers led through lush, colorful plantings and recreational areas. The family could enjoy a croquet lawn, a tennis pavilion, a nine-hole golf course, a wading pool, shady pergolas and grottoes, a summerhouse, and a teahouse. The gardens were decorated with statuary and rough local stone embellished with colorful Rookwood tiles of the Arts and Crafts period.

In 1949 Peter P. Blanchard, Jr., purchased the property, and he and his wife, Adelaide Childs Frick, brought a more restrained classical formality to the estate. They replaced the flamboyant

house with a Georgian brick mansion, and supplanted the extravagant flower beds with simple hedges of boxwood and yew and allées of London plane and spruce trees.

In 2000, following his father's wishes, Peter P. Blanchard III and his wife, Sofia, began restoring the garden to its early 1900s appearance. They converted it to a nonprofit conservation organization with assistance from the Garden Conservancy. The garden needed extensive work before it opened to the public in 2013. The walls, terraces, stairs, pools, statuary, and colonnades all had to be repaired. Trees and hedges were pruned or removed, and 28 acres of formal and naturalistic gardens were restored.

Today's Greenwood Gardens combines historic features with contemporary planting schemes. Visitors arrive through an entrance drive lined with London plane trees. The Forecourt garden is planted with native dogwoods, Hinoki cypress, rhododendrons, and heathers with swaths of Pennsylvania sedge for a modern feel. Two pavilions flank the house, one of which is home to the magnificent Bird of Paradise wrought iron gate.

In the back of the house, the Upper Terrace is designed for outdoor entertaining with wisteria-covered pergolas, comfortable benches, Majolica vases and statuary. Spring bulbs, flowering trees, and uncommon shrubs and perennials provide color from spring through fall. A sweeping view of the recently restored Main Axis garden reveals the D-shaped reflecting pool ringed with perennials, the croquet lawn, and the Garden of the Gods with its signature green trellises.

Parallel to the Main Axis is a walkway lined with boxwood, rhododendrons, viburnums and eclectic garden sculptures and ornaments. Swaths of epimediums, corydalis and hellebores thrive on this shady pathway. You will encounter several

enchanting follies including the octahedral Summer House shaded by 100-year old horse chestnut trees; the Tea House with its Rookwood-studded ceiling; and the Cascade with its seven-tier, gravity fed fountain.

Reeves-Reed Arboretum

165 Hobart Ave., Summit, NJ 07901
908-273-8787
reeves-reedarboretum.org

AREA: 13.5 acres

HOURS: April –Oct. : daily 7–7; Nov.–March: daily 9–4

ADMISSION: Suggested donation $5

AMENITIES:

EVENTS: Seasonal festivals, educational programs, art exhibits, concerts

Reeves-Reed Arboretum began as a country retreat called The Clearing built by John Hornor Wisner in 1889. Wisner hired Calvert Vaux, a partner of Frederick Law Olmsted, to create an overall plan for the estate. Vaux designed a pastoral landscape that took advantage of the natural scenery and its views of the New York City skyline. The property's unique feature was "the bowl" a large, steep-sided depression created by a glacier more than 17,000 years ago. The Wisners sledded and skied in the bowl, and Isabella Wisner planted the first daffodil bulbs that are now a major Arboretum attraction.

In 1916, new owners Richard and Susie Graham Reeves transformed the gardens in the fashion of the Country Place era. They replaced the kitchen garden and laundry yard with a series of formal gardens. Susie expanded the daffodil collection

with tens of thousands of bulbs, and commissioned landscape architects Ellen Biddle Shipman and Carl F. Pilat to refine the plantings.

The resulting gardens are a beautifully maintained example of early 20th century landscape architecture. Elegant stone steps lead to a landscape of themed garden rooms. Three of the gardens have been returned as closely as possible to their original appearance: the Azalea Garden, the Rose Garden, and the Rock Garden. During the Reeves' tenure, what is now called the Azalea Garden was simply the Flower Garden, planted with biennials and perennials in yellow, blue, and purple. It was the focal point of the property, where Susie spent much of her time and energy, and where her daughter was married in 1940. The bluestone borders in the lawn of the current Azalea Garden mark the outlines of the flowerbeds that were later abandoned due to the cost and labor of maintaining them.

The Rose Garden, installed around 1925, displays 286 rose bushes representing more than 150 varieties of floribundas and hybrid teas, laid out in a traditional circle-in-a-square design. Susie exhibited her roses at the New Jersey Rose Show in nearby Morristown, where she was reportedly "showered with honors." Old-fashioned roses flank the formal garden, and climbing roses are trained on posts and chains. The adjacent Rock Garden with its pool and waterfall once featured sun-loving alpine plants. Now it is a shady retreat and an inviting habitat for birds.

In 1968, the Charles L. Reed family became the estate's last private owners, adding the patterned herb garden and opening woodland trails. In 1974 the Arboretum became a public garden managed by the city of Summit.

The Arboretum is a prime destination in April, when more than 50,000 daffodils bloom. After

they fade, the bowl is a meadow for wildlife. A two-level Perennial Border overlooks the bowl, with epimediums, amsonias, anemones, alliums, and baptisias. An Island Garden in the parking area is planted with billowy plants in soft colors for late summer—grasses, agastache, perovskia, and caryopteris. Interesting tree specimens line the perimeter of the parking lot, including paper-bark maple, *Parrottia persica,* and a large plum yew. The Arboretum's collection includes katsura, sourwood, bald cypress, giant sequoia, and *Frank-linia* trees, as well as a sugar maple, purple beech, and three 100-year-old ginkgos.

Colonial Park Gardens

156 Mettlers Rd., Somerset, NJ 08873
908-722-1200 x5008
somersetcountyparks.org/colonial-park-gardens

AREA: 144 acres

HOURS: Daily sunrise–sunset

ADMISSION: $6 suggested donation

AMENITIES:

EVENTS: Rose Day Festival

Located on the western end of a large county park with a myriad of recreational areas, Colonia Park Gardens is a plant lover's delight. It includes an award-winning rose garden, a nationally accredited arboretum, a perennial garden, a Fragrance and Sensory Garden, and other horticultural collections.

The rose garden and surrounding arboretum were once part of the Mettler estate, a working farm with formal gardens surrounding the house. The flagstone walks and small stone pool are original to the estate. The one-acre Rudolf W. van der Goot Rose Garden is named after Somerset County's first horticulturist and features more than 3,000 roses of 325 varieties. You will find popular modern hybrids, species roses, climbers, tree roses, polyanthas, and floribundas in a kaleidoscope of color, form, and fragrance. There

is a Grandmother's Garden, planted with roses popular before World War II. The Dutch Garden is designed in a formal style of raised beds framed by low growing perennials. Of special interest is the collection of old garden roses: Albas, Bourbons, Centifolias, Chinas, Damasks, Mosses, and Noisettes that delight gardeners with their strong perfume and lush, cabbage-shaped blooms. Their names alone—'Königin von Dänemark,' 'Petite de Hollande,' 'Marchesa Boccella,' 'Madame Isaac Péreire'— transport you to another continent and century.

Adjacent to the rose garden is the Fragrance and Sensory Garden, which was designed for visitors with visual or physical disabilities. It is an interactive garden that invites visitors to touch textured plants such as the rubbery sedum, spiky blue fescue and downy lamb's ear; smell the perfume of lavender, jasmine, basil, mint, thyme, and scented geranium; and enjoy the view of brightly colored flowers. This sunken garden is surrounded by a stone wall and built with raised beds that provide easy access to the plants.

Redesigned in 2019, the four acre perennial garden encircles a welcoming gazebo. The garden comes to life in early spring with grape hyacinths and daffodils and provides color through autumn with ornamental grasses and colorful foliage. The perennials are accented by hollies, lilacs, weigelas, ninebarks and other ornamental shrubs and trees. The park's arboretum showcases more than 900 varieties of trees and shrubs. While many are native to the United States, you will find specimens from Europe, Asia, Africa, South America, and the Middle East.

Rutgers Gardens

Rutgers University, 130 Log Cabin Rd., New Brunswick, NJ 08901
848-932-7000
rutgersgardens.rutgers.edu

AREA: 180 acres

HOURS: Tues.–Sun. 8–5

ADMISSION: Free

EVENTS: Spring Flower Fair, plant sales, community events, and workshops

For more than 100 years, Rutgers Gardens has served as a living laboratory for Rutgers University faculty, staff, and students. It is also a dynamic botanic garden consisting of plant collections, themed gardens, and natural habitats with a student-run farm and farmers market for the community. In recent years the focus has been on providing display gardens and educational programs for the home gardener.

You will find many themed gardens on the property, including a Succulent Garden of eastern prickly pears, stonecrops, aloes, sansevierias, and agaves; a Pollinator Garden with varieties of bee balm, milkweed, ironweed, baptisia, viburnum, and sumac; and an All-America Selections Garden that evaluates new cultivars of annuals, vegetables, and perennials for home gardens. Other interesting features include the two-acre Bamboo Grove, with a winding path and footbridge over a

small stream. This stand of *Phyllostachys nuda* was originally planted in the 1940s as a wind screen for honeybee colonies.

In late summer the Donald B. Lacey Display Garden provides a dazzling show of colorful annuals, tropicals, herbs, and vegetables. Arranged in a formal pattern of concentric squares around an ornamental pond, this garden showcases new varieties in bold combinations. In the spring this display garden dazzles with a display of 14,000 grape hyacinths, daffodils, and crown imperials (*Fritillaria imperialis.*) In the summer, cannas, verbenas, cleomes, zinnias, and many other tropicals accented with ornamental grasses and vegetables in designs that change every year. Three perennial borders in shades of red, blue, yellow, and purple, dubbed the "chroma beds," frame the annual and bulb display.

Adjacent to the Lacey Display Garden is the Roy H. DeBoer Evergreen Garden, named after the founder of the Landscape Architecture program at Rutgers. Most of the cedars, pines, spruces, and firs were planted in the 1950s around the great sunken lawn. A large weeping white pine (*Pinus strobus* 'Pendula') serves as the focal point of this tranquil garden.

The Rain Garden is another valuable educational tool for the public. Such gardens are designed to reduce stormwater runoff from impermeable surfaces such as driveways, parking lots, and rooftops. Pollutants in the water are removed via the absorption and metabolism by plants. Trees such as river birch, fringe tree, and sweetbay magnolia planted near the Rain Garden help to absorb excess water, while water-loving sedges, ferns, milkweeds, Joe Pye weed, lobelias, and irises mitigate the stormwater runoff.

As part of a research institution, Rutgers Gardens encompasses several plant breeding programs,

research projects, and collections of individual species. When the gardens were founded more than 100 years ago, the earliest breeding programs focused on peaches, hollies, and dogwoods. Thanks to the research of renowned plant breeder Dr. Elwin Orton, Rutgers Gardens features one of the largest holly display gardens in the country, with many unique hybrids of our native Ameri-can holly. Dr. Orton also took on the challenge of developing disease-resistant dogwoods by crossing native eastern flowering dogwood (*Cornus florida*) with the Asian *Cornus kousa*. The result is a collection of beautiful Stellar dogwood hybrids released in the 1990s that include 'Aurora,' 'Constellation,' 'Celestial,' and 'Stellar Pink' and are popular with gardeners all over the country.

Cross Estate Gardens

61 Jockey Hollow Rd., Bernardsville, NJ 07924
908-766-1699
crossestategardens.org

AREA: 5 acres of gardens

HOURS: Daily 8 am–sunset

ADMISSION: Suggested donation $8

EVENTS: Plant sale in May, garden tours Wednesdays from mid-April–October, 10 & 11:30 am

The Cross Estate Gardens date to the early 20th century when grand country mansions were built as summer retreats in the Mountain Colony of Bernardsville. Between 1903 and 1906, Ella and John Anderson Bensel assembled some 300 acres of property which they named Queen Anne Farm and built a 23-room stone house and outbuildings.

A civil engineer, Bensel was familiar with water systems. So it is no surprise that when he built his isolated summer villa, he added a water tower to make it self-sufficient. Capped with a wooden windmill, the five-story tower dominated the landscape and afforded scenic views of the countryside. Now restored, it once again provides water for the estate buildings and gardens.

In 1929, William Redmond Cross purchased the estate and renamed it Hardscrabble House. His wife, Julia Appleton Newbold Cross, was the daughter of Thomas and Sarah Newbold of Bellefield, whose garden had been designed by Beatrix Farrand. She would become president of the Horticultural Society of New York in the 1950s. With the help of landscape architects Clarence Fowler and her friend Martha Brookes Hutcheson, Julia made extensive improvements to the property and cultivated an unusual assortment of plants. She created a sunken walled parterre garden planted with annuals, and a natural garden of wildflowers planted in drifts among serpentine pathways. This pairing of formal gardens and woodland gardens was a favorite aspect of early 20th century landscape design.

In 1975, 162 acres of the property, including the primary buildings, were added to the Morristown National Historical Park. The addition provided assured protection for the adjacent 18th century New Jersey Brigade Revolutionary War encampment area. Funds were not available to maintain the gardens, which soon fell into disrepair, and in 1977 local residents began a volunteer project to revive them. Paths and walkways were uncovered and vegetation was removed, pruned, or replaced. Dedicated volunteers continue to work in the garden every Wednesday from March to December. Their diligent effort has preserved a fine example of a Country Plae era garden for others to enjoy.

Julia Cross's restored gardens are the star of the estate. The formal walled garden, created on two levels, features exciting combinations of perennials. May is an excellent time to see the tree peonies and the purple and white wisteria that adorns the stone pergola. In the neighboring wild garden, native shrubs and wildflowers are in bloom.

Peony's Envy

34 Autumn Hill Rd., Bernardsville, NJ 07924
908-578-3032
peonysenvy.com

HOURS: Last Friday in April–second Sunday in June:
daily 11–5
ADMISSION: $10
AMENITIES: 🏺
EVENTS: Friday night picnics, Peak Bloom Party

If you're driving through New Jersey in the late spring, you must visit the world's largest public peony garden—Peony's Envy in Bernardsville.

Peony's Envy is home to more than 700 varieties of tree, herbaceous, and intersectional peonies that enjoy cult status among aficionados. The seven-acre production garden is also a beautiful display garden, with formal flower beds, stone walls, and meandering paths through the woodland.

The bloom sequence begins with the woodland and tree peonies, which open in early May. Many gardeners are unfamiliar with woodland peonies (*Paeonia Japonica*) that prefer the early spring sun and summer shade of deciduous woodlands. These peonies sport delicate creamy white blooms in spring, lush summer foliage, and dramatic scar-

let seedpods in fall. The 2,000 tree peonies at the nursery also prefer dappled sunlight, and produce dinner-plate-sized flowers. They are long-lasting woody shrubs from China and Tibet that can grow to seven feet. The nursery's herbaceous peonies bloom for a span of about four weeks, beginning with the fern leaf and coral varieties, followed by pink, white, and magenta. The last to bloom are the intersectional peonies—hybrids of tree and herbaceous peonies that come in many colors, including yellow.

During bloom season, hundreds of visitors flock to the garden daily. Owner Kathleen Gagan is welcoming and enthusiastic, and offers excellent advice to novice and experienced gardeners alike. If you miss the spring bloom season, Peony's Envy reopens again in the fall for bare-root sales, and peonies can be ordered via mail order from September to May. The nursery's extensive website is an excellent resource.

Willowwood Arboretum

14 Longview Rd., Far Hills, NJ 07931
908-234-1815
morrisparks.net

AREA: 30 acres

HOURS: Daily 8 am–sunset

ADMISSION: Free

AMENITIES: 👫

EVENTS: Lectures, public programs

The Willowwood Arboretum is a historic farmstead that became home to three extraordinary horticulturists—brothers Robert and Henry Wells Tubbs and Professor Benjamin Blackburn. Today it is operated by the Morris County Park Commission with support from the Willowwood Foundation, which are devoted to preserving the garden and educating the public about botany and environmental science.

The 135-acre farmstead was purchased in 1908 by the Tubbs brothers, enthusiastic gardeners who had professional careers in New York City. On the property were a farmhouse and several outbuildings. Massive willows lined a brook there, so they named it Willowwood Farm. The brothers' parents and sister joined them at the farm, and the entire family set to work. Ardent plant collectors, the Tubbs brothers developed relationships with renowned horticulturists and plant hunters

including Ernest Henry Wilson, Charles Sprague Sargent, and their neighbor Martha Brookes Hutcheson. She introduced them to Professor Benjamin Blackburn, an instructor in Ornamental Horticulture at Rutgers and Drew universities, who joined them in collecting plants and developing the gardens into a curated arboretum. Blackburn eventually became owner of Willowwood, and deeded it to the Morris County Park Commission upon his death in 1987.

You approach Willowwood on a long drive winding through the bucolic Long Meadow blooming with daffodils in the spring and wildflowers in summer. A wisteria-draped pergola welcomes you to a cluster of historic barns. Three formal gardens surround the Tubbs's house. The Cottage Garden, with its decorative wrought-iron gate, has colorful flower beds with perennials and spring bulbs on both sides of a stone pathway punctuated by slender cypresses. The back porch of the house offers views of Pan's Garden, with a bust of the Greek god Pan and a tapestry of plants in the pattern of a Persian prayer rug. The Mediterranean-style Rosary juxtaposes bold foliage and bright color. To the right of the house, towering bald cypresses and Japanese maples provide a shady retreat for an Asian-inspired garden with a woodland pool and waterfall.

The collector's spirit is evident throughout—from the orchards of flowering cherries and mature zelkovas, to the groves of lilacs, the giant Dawn Redwood, the numerous magnolias and viburnums, and the exotic conifers and trees with intriguing bark in the Winter Garden. Epimediums, hostas, tree peonies, orchids, and unusual perennials delight casual and sophisticated gardeners alike. Willowwood is a pleasure to visit in all seasons.

Bamboo Brook Outdoor Education Ctr.

11 Longview Rd., Far Hills, NJ 07931
973-326-7600
morrisparks.net

AREA: 100 acres

HOURS: Daily 8 am–sunset

ADMISSION: Free

AMENITIES: 👫

EVENTS: Various events through Park Commission; self-guided cell phone tour

Bamboo Brook Outdoor Education Center was once known as Merchiston Farm and was the home of landscape architect Martha Brookes Hutcheson and her husband from 1911 to 1959. Hutcheson was one of America's first female landscape architects. She attended the School of Architecture and Planning at the Massachusetts Institute of Technology along with Marion Coffin and Beatrix Farrand. Hutcheson's design for Merchiston Farm was completed shortly after the publication of her book *The Spirit of the Garden*, in 1923.

Hutcheson's European travels inspired her to design the garden in the Beaux-Arts style popular in the early 20th century. Drawing on European Renaissance and Baroque gardens as well as those of Islamic-era Spain, Beaux-Arts gardens used formal geometry, allées and hedges, long vistas, reflecting pools and fountains, and native plants and materials. You see these design principles immediately when you enter Bamboo Brook's circular drive punctuated with white dogwoods underplanted with green hostas and white daffodils. Hutcheson used a restrained color palette and repeated the circle motif throughout her landscape.

The path from the driveway leads to the Upper Water—a pond designed to appear as a naturalized body of water. It was placed to take advantage of both the topography and the architecture of the house, and, importantly, it reflects the plants, the house, and the sky. A winding stream leads from the Upper Water to the rest of the garden. Hutcheson was fascinated with water features and constructed an intricate system of cisterns, pipes, swales, and catch basins to supply her house, pools, and gardens with collected rainwater.

The East Lawn and Coffee Terrace were designed with formal axial geometry. Informal plantings circle the oval East Lawn, which connects to the Circular Pool. The Circular Pool was originally a farm pond in a natural hollow which provided

water for livestock. It was transformed into a reflecting pool with six radiating paths and plantings of iris, phlox, ferns, dogwoods, and vinca.

Beyond the lawn lies an axial garden with a white cedar allée and parterres adjacent to a former tennis court and the children's playhouse. Hutcheson placed rustic wood benches and chairs at spots where views could be enjoyed. She adapted native plants such as dogwood, sweet pepperbush, and elderberry to an Italian Renaissance-inspired design, and used local stone to create walls, patios, and steps throughout the garden.

The Little House was Hutcheson's quiet getaway. It was built over a small stream, which Hutcheson embellished with spillways and a lily pool, providing a home for water lovers such as sweetfern and iris.

A straight road lined with elms and oaks extends from the house to a farm complex with a farmhouse, barn, garage, and various work yards set in an informal landscape of fields and woods.

In 1972 Hutcheson's heirs gave the property to the Morris County Park Commission, and it has been restored to its 1945 appearance. In addition to the formal areas, there are numerous trails that wind through the fields and along Bamboo Brook, and connect to the Elizabeth D. Kay Environmental Center and Willowwood Arboretum.

Leonard J. Buck Garden

11 Layton Rd., Far Hills, NJ 07931
908-722-1200 x5011
somersetcountyparks.org/leonard-j-buck-garden

AREA: 33 acres
HOURS: Mon. –Fri. 10–4, Sat .10–5, Sun. 12–5; closed major holidays & weekends Dec.–March
ADMISSION: Suggested donation $7
AMENITIES:
EVENTS: Lectures, public programs

The Leonard J. Buck Garden is one of the finest and largest rock gardens in the eastern United States. It consists of a series of alpine and woodland gardens situated in a 33-acre wooded stream valley. While most rock gardens are man-made and small in scale like the alpine plants they showcase, this rock garden is a series of huge natural rock outcroppings in a 500-foot-wide, 90-foot-deep gorge. The gorge was formed at the end of the Ice Age, about 12,000 years ago, when the water from melting glaciers carved out the valley of Moggy Hollow.

The rocky garden backbone was perfect for Leonard Buck, a geologist who made his fortune in mining. As he traveled the world on business, he collected rare plants. In the 1930s Buck was a trustee of the New York Botanical Garden, where he met and hired Swiss-born landscape architect Zenon Schreiber. The duo set out to develop a naturalistic woodland garden composed of many smaller gardens, each with its own character and microhabitat.

Buck and Schreiber worked by eye and proportion, without a formal plan on paper. Buck worked the rock—chiseling, picking, and shoveling to expose the rugged face. Schreiber worked the plants, tucking in rare and exotic specimens among the stones. He planted azaleas and rhododendrons at the base of the valley walls to create a dazzling display in spring. He also established a backbone of dogwoods, crabapples, shadbush, fothergilla, viburnums, and other native trees and shrubs throughout the property.

When Interstate 287 was being laid out, the original plans called for the highway to run directly through Buck's property. Buck invited the officials in charge to visit his garden and succeeded in having the interstate rerouted. After his death in 1976, the family donated the garden to the Somerset County Park Commission and set up a trust to fund maintenance and renovations.

The garden's trails wind past two ponds and a rock-edged stream, through the woods, and up into the gorge. At its spring peak, the garden is a showcase for lady slippers, trilliums, woodland phloxes, bergenias, *Iris cristatas*, tiarellas, epimediums, and columbines. Siberian squill, Spanish bluebells, winter aconites, grape hyacinths, and other miniature bulbs enchance the floral display. Japanese primroses line the streambed and masses of azaleas dazzle in the valley. To help plan your visit, the garden website provides a weekly list of plants in bloom. There is something to see in every season.

Duke Farms

1112 Dukes Parkway West, Hillsborough, NJ 08844
908-722-3700
dukefarms.org

AREA: 1,000 acres
HOURS: Closed Sun. & Mon. See website for hours
ADMISSION: Free, entry passes required on Saturday
AMENITIES: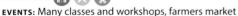
EVENTS: Many classes and workshops, farmers market

With more than 1,000 acres open to the public, Duke Farms is a nature sanctuary in the most populous state in the country. What was once a Gilded Age estate is now a center for environmental stewardship, offering myriad opportunities for visitors to enjoy nature.

Tobacco and hydropower magnate James Buchanan Duke purchased the original 372-acre farm in 1893. He acquired 40 additional farmsteads to create a 2,700-acre estate with a working farm. Duke envisioned a grand public garden on the site and enhanced the landscape with a series of lakes, bridges, fountains, and waterfalls. His daughter Doris further developed the gardens during her lifetime. Doris was also an avid environmentalist and stipulated that upon her death Duke Farms would be maintained as a wildlife refuge and horticultural research facility. That directive created the Duke Farms that you experience today.

The property features 20 miles of walking and bi-

cycle trails through diverse habitats, an arboretum of specimen trees, several lakes, and a four-mile stretch of the Raritan River to enjoy. Programming includes educational workshops about the environment and wildlife conservation, volunteering opportunities for habitat restoration, a community garden, and seasonal farmers market.

Architectural remnants of the Gilded Age estate form the backbone of contemporary gardens. Close to the entrance you will find the remains of the Hay Barn, which was once the center of farming activity. After a fire in 1915, Doris transformed the ruins into an outdoor gallery of marble figurative statues set in a collection of lilacs. The Old Foundation was the building site of the formal mansion on the estate that was never completed. It overlooks an open space that was originally designed as a Great Lawn. Today it is a naturalistic meadow of native grasses and wildflowers that are home to birds and pollinators. A red Japanese bridge, Korean dog statues, and stone lanterns form the Meditation Garden. This was once Doris's Asian-style garden, with plantings of dogwoods, cherries, Japanese maples, and redbuds surrounding a stream with a waterfall.

Built in 1901, the Orchid Range was the estate's first conservatory, housing palms, poinsettias, roses, cacti, and tropical plants. Doris was keenly interested in orchids and most of the moth orchids available today are hybrids of *Phalaeonopsis* 'Doris' developed at Duke Farms. Today the Orchid Range is a LEED-certified greenhouse home to conservation programs focused on endangered tropical plants and local plant species.

Paths guide you around seven lakes that were created by J. B. Duke in 1909 and reflected his interest in hydropower. These lakes were excavated with steam-powered engines and a huge crew of workers with mule teams. The excavated soil was mounded throughout the property to create knolls

and hills and frame lovely vistas. One million gallons of water per day were pumped from the Raritan River to Duke Reservoir, where the water was released to flow by gravity through the seven-lake system and back into the Raritan River. You will also find the Great Falls, a tiered waterfall located off the side of Duke Reservoir. The falls run from April to October at 10 am, 12 pm, 2 pm, and 4 pm.

Morven Museum & Garden

55 Stockton St., Princeton, NJ 08540
609-924-8144 x103
morven.org

AREA: 5 acres

HOURS: Wed.–Sun. 10–4

ADMISSION: $10

AMENITIES: 🌳 👪 🏛️

EVENTS: Morven in May Weekend, Spring Plant Sale

Richard and Annis Stockton

The Morven Museum & Garden has an illustrious 270-year history as the home of a Revolutionary patriot and of five New Jersey governors. It was built in the 1750s by Richard Stockton on property granted to his grandfather by William Penn. Stockton was a prominent lawyer and signer of the Declaration of Independence. His wife, Annis Boudinot Stockton, referred to as "the elegant Muse of Morven" by George Washington, was one of America's earliest female poets. The two-and-a-half-story brick mansion served as the home of the Stockton family until 1944, when it became the first Governor's Mansion in New Jersey.

The gardens at Morven were influenced by many generations of the Stockton family as well as by the changing fashions of landscape design. Richard "The Signer" purchased the land between Morven and Stockton Street to create an impressive entry to his mansion. He planted a row of 13 catalpa trees along the new boundary, representing each of the newly declared states. Annis created the formal terraced gardens behind the house with beds devoted to different plants. She also designed a grotto decorated with seashells. Annis described the homestead's orchards of apples, peaches, plums, cherries, and pears in her writings. Their son Richard "The Duke" boasted that his cider was as fine as wine. He also designed the present horseshoe-shaped drive and paved forecourt in front of the house.

Subsequent generations of Stocktons had great interest in the gardens. In the 1850s, Robert Field "Commodore" Stockton erected a heated greenhouse for his lemon trees, cacti, azaleas, daphnes, and camellias. His extensive plant collections

and greenhouse reflected his refinement, stature, and financial standing in the community. By this time, the entrance garden had become a curvilinear front lawn dotted with ornamental trees in the "picturesque" style. The beautiful wisteria that drapes across the front portico was added in the 1880s. With the emergence of the Colonial Revival Movement in the late 1800s, Helen Hamilton Shields Stockton restored the formal gardens. She collected cuttings from gardens at home and abroad, including sweet Williams from Abbotsford, hollyhocks from Kew Gardens, and other flowers from Dow Castle, Sandringham, and Cliveden.

Morven underwent extensive restoration and reopened as a museum and garden in 2004. Two floors of galleries showcase the stories of the people who lived and worked at Morven through the centuries. The five-acre site includes the mansion, wash and ice house, carriage house, pool house, and restored historic gardens. The gardens reflect the Colonial Revival period with boxwood hedges and formal flower beds of historic peonies, lilies, phloxes, and irises punctuated by a classical white arbor. Peonies grow in abundance throughout the property, lining the front facade of the house as well as the historic brick wall. Erected in the 1850s to separate the service yard from ornamental landscaping, the wall is covered in climbing roses, clematis, and climbing hydrangeas.

Prospect House and Garden

Princeton University, Washington St., Princeton, NJ 08544
609-258-3455

AREA: 5 acres

HOURS: Daily dawn–dusk

ADMISSION: Free

AMENITIES:

Prospect House stands on the Princeton University campus, located between the art museum and Washington Street. It was built in 1851 for Thomas Fuller Potter and designed by John Notman, a Scottish architect who introduced the Italianate style of architecture to the United States. The handsome sandstone mansion features a three-story tower and a porte cochere topped by a decorative balustrade. The property was gifted to Princeton University, then known as the College of New Jersey, in 1878, and for the next 90 years served as the residence of the college president. It was designated a National Historic Landmark in 1985 and now serves as the private clubhouse for university faculty.

President Woodrow Wilson lived at Prospect House from 1902 to 1911, first as college president and then as governor of New Jersey. His first wife Ellen was an artist and designed the lush garden surrounding the mansion. When viewed from above, the garden's pathways defined the outlines of the shield in the university's seal. Within those outlines, thousands of annuals provided color in the garden from spring through fall.

In 2012 Prospect House garden was redesigned by renowned landscape architects Lynden B. Miller and Ronda M. Brands. The plantings were transitioned from what was primarily an annuals display to a mix of shrubs, perennials, bulbs, and annuals. This mixed style of planting complements the style of other gardens found on the campus and is more sustainable. The focal point of the garden is a grouping of four narrow arborvitae that frame a fountain on a central axis from the house. Maroon barberries and golden spireas provide long-lasting color at the base of the sculptural trees. Yew and boxwood hedges form a strong structural framework for the colorful flowers. In the spring thousands of tulips in shades of red, yellow, and pink dazzle in the garden. These are followed by the blooms of peonies, irises, baptisias, daylilies, and hydrangeas accented with annuals.

While the garden has been shaped and changed over the years, many of its trees predate the house. There are lovely old specimens of tulip trees, American beeches, yews, hawthorns, and cedars of Lebanon. Surrounding the flower garden is a shady walk lined with rhododendrons, azaleas, mountain laurels, and hollies underplanted with ivy and hostas. Benches provide a tranquil setting for studying or enjoying the garden.

The entire Princeton University campus reflects the work of Beatrix Jones Farrand, the university's first consulting landscape architect and a powerful force in shaping the look of the campus from 1912 to 1943. Farrand's designs included beautiful vistas and native plants and trees, particularly varieties that bloom in spring or fall when the university is in session. Her timeless approach to the landscape is still evident today.

Deep Cut Gardens

152 Red Hill Rd., Middletown, NJ 07748
732-671-6050
monmouthcountyparks.com

AREA: 54 acres
HOURS: Daily 8 am–dusk
ADMISSION: Free admission
AMENITIES:
EVENTS: Plant swaps, gardening programs

Deep Cut Gardens was named after the rivulet that makes its way through the sloped property. The gardens were established by mafioso Vito Genovese, who owned the property from 1935 to 1947. Genovese wanted a garden that would evoke his homeland of Naples, Italy. He hired landscape architect Theodore Stout to create "something big enough to make an impression from the top of the hill," and gave him free reign.

Since the original Colonial Revival mansion did not fully lend itself to an Italianate garden, Stout's design mixed English and Italian styles. The property had adequate water for the terraced pools of traditional Italian gardens, so an elaborate rockery was constructed. Three cascading pools were encircled with volcanic rock that was allegedly imported from Italy at Genovese's request. These pools were dry and quiet for years, but have recently been refurbished. The sound of trickling water brings a delightfully cooling effect to this part of the garden. Ancient Sargent's weeping hemlocks form a shady green canopy over the cascading pools, which have been planted with ferns and other shade lovers.

Terraced gardens at the foot of the hillside are planted with heaths, heathers, and other rockery plants. Genovese's special requirement for the garden was a stone Vesuvius, complete with space for a fire inside the mountain's belly, and Stout filled the request on the left side of the hill. The rise provides a perfect vantage point to view the large, recessed parterre garden below. Surrounded by a low stone wall and anchored by a masonry pergola, the garden contains colorful roses and perennials.

Only two years after he purchased the property, Genovese left the United States to avoid arrest, and an unexplained fire destroyed his mansion. The property was eventually purchased by Karl and Marjorie Sperry Wihtol, who built the existing house and renovated the greenhouse and the gardens. In 1977 they donated Deep Cut Farm to the Monmouth County Park System to be used as a park and horticultural destination. The county began restoring the parterre in 2005. Years of design and preparation went into transforming the landscape to its 1930s appearance. The 180 rose bushes, perennials, and the surrounding boxwoods where planted in 2008.

Today, Deep Cut Gardens is dedicated to the home gardener. The 54 acres of gardens and greenhouses are a living catalog of cultivated and native plants to be observed through the seasons. To the historic gardens the county has added a butterfly and hummingbird garden, lily pond, shade garden, azalea and rhododendron walk, dried-flower production field, vegetable gardens, and the All-American Test Garden, which features new varieties of annuals, perennials and vegetables. In the spring, 1,400 tulips create a stunning display. Beyond the formal gardens, walking paths wind

through the meadows and groves of chestnuts, oaks, maples, and ash, and around a natural pond. One of the site's year-round attractions is the 1,950-square-foot greenhouse Genovese installed, which showcases cacti, bonsai trees, orchids, succulents, and collections of tender plants.

Sayen House & Gardens

155 Hughes Dr., Hamilton Square, NJ 08690
609-890-3630
hamiltonnj.com/sayengardens

AREA: 30 acres

HOURS: Daily dawn–dusk

ADMISSION: Free

AMENITIES: 👥 👶

EVENTS: Mother's Day Azalea Festival

Sayen House & Gardens is a 30-acre horticultural oasis tucked into a busy suburb. A public park since 1991, Sayen has been a haven for gardeners, birdwatchers, walkers, and anyone seeking a peaceful outdoor refuge.

Frederick and Anne Mellon Sayen purchased the parcel in 1912 to build their home. The site was close to the family rubber mill in Hamilton Square. They built an Arts and Crafts style bungalow and began laying out the garden. Frederick was an avid gardener and world traveler. As he traveled, he collected ornamental plants, principally from China, Japan, and England. Many of those plants flourish in the garden today, including more than 1,000 azaleas and 500 rhododendrons. These shrubs form the backbone of the horticulture collection, lining walkways and forming colorful backdrops for gazebos and other seating areas.

From the entrance, you can take several paths that lead through island plantings of shrubs, conifers, and specimen trees. The paths curve around ponds and streams lined with yellow irises and crossed by picturesque bridges. Spring unveils a magnificent display of color and beauty with more than 250,000 flowering daffodils, tulips, crocuses, and other bulbs. A visit in early May is particularly stunning, with hundreds of azaleas, rhododendrons, viburnums, and dogwoods in peak bloom. These are underplanted with bleeding hearts, amsonias, columbines, and other spring perennials. By the end of May, you will see peonies blooming as well as roses, impatiens, and clematis. Numerous gazebos and pergolas create lovely places to sit and enjoy the colors and scents of the garden.

The south end of the property is LaBaw Pointe, which has been designed in a more naturalistic style. Here you will find a small frog pond with a waterfall and plantings of river birch, weeping willows, magnolias, and fringe trees with their delicate white flowers. The 1.3-mile walking trail winds through the entire property of gardens and natural woodlands.

Grounds for Sculpture

80 Sculptors Way, Hamilton, NJ 08619
609-586-0616
groundsforsculpture.org

AREA: 42 acres

HOURS: Wed. –Mon. 10–6; timed tickets required

ADMISSION: $25

AMENITIES:

EVENTS: Changing exhibitions and art, horticulture and wellness programs

Nestled in the heart of central New Jersey is Grounds for Sculpture, where art and nature come together to form a magical place. This open-air sculpture park, arboretum and museum exhibits more than 300 sculptures by renowned and emerging contemporary artists, each thoughtfully positioned within a meticulously landscaped park full of thousands of trees and flowers.

The brainchild of prolific sculptor J. Seward Johnson, Grounds for Sculpture opened in 1992 on the site of the former New Jersey State Fairgrounds. Johnson's desire was to make contemporary sculpture accessible to people from all backgrounds in an informal setting. His own iconic life-size bronze sculptures are found throughout the park—among them, his *Beyond the Frame* series based on Impressionist paintings. You can join Renoir's "Luncheon of the Boating Party," traverse Monet's "Bridge over a Pond of Water Lilies," or sit

in on Manet's "Le Dejeuner sur l'herbe."

The permanent collection at Grounds for Sculpture includes works by such distinguished artists as Clement Meadmore, Anthony Caro, Beverly Pepper, Kiki Smith, George Segal, Magdalena Abakanowicz, and Isaac Witkin. Rotating special exhibitions of artists from all over the world supplement the permanent collection.

From the start, Grounds for Sculpture paid equal attention to both artwork and site. Hills, valleys, and waterways surround various sculptures. The setting of each sculpture is determined by a collaboration of a curator, horticulturist, and artist, so that each piece is beautifully integrated in the garden. The resulting juxtaposition of art and nature provides an amazing aesthetic experience for the visitor.

The landscaping at Grounds for Sculpture incorporates more than 2,000 trees, as well as shrubs, perennial gardens, ponds, courtyards, terraces, and pergolas. You can walk through a bamboo forest, sit in a quiet enclosure, admire hundreds of lotus blooms in a pond, and walk through a wisteria-draped pergola. Everywhere you turn, delightful sculpted tableaus provide the sense that you are playing a role in the scene. Open areas display large sculptures that invite interaction. A surprise is around every corner, and most visitors walk through the gardens with smiles on their faces.

The fantasyland environment is a fabulous introduction to art for children. Life-like sculptures, giant xylophones, tiny mazes, and tree tunnels form a natural playground, and peacocks wander the property. You can spend a day here, enjoying the six indoor galleries, museum shop, and special programs, and have lunch at one of the two cafés, or dinner at the fine-dining option, Rat's Restaurant.

RareFind Nursery

957 Patterson Rd., Jackson, NJ 08527
732-833-0613, support@rarefindnursery.com
rarefindnursery.com

HOURS: By appointment only
AMENITIES:

"If you can find it in a garden center, we probably don't have it!" Hank Schannen said of the nursery he founded in 1998. Since that time, RareFind Nursery has stayed true to its mission, providing unusual and special plants.

Although he spent his career in marketing research, Schannen's passion was rhododendrons. He collected unusual varieties on the West Coast and in Europe, bred his own hybrids, and was an active member of the American Rhododendron Society. Schannen was fondly called "the Ambassador," a nickname that expressed his love and enthusiasm for the genus. Although he passed away in 2009, RareFind nursery continues to offer an impressive selection of rhododendrons and azaleas, including some of Schannen's hybrids.

RareFind operates primarily as a mail-order business, with an impressive following nationwide. Special collections you will find there are witch hazels, magnolias (including unusual yellow-flowered varieties), hydrangeas, and carnivorous and bog plants. There is also a great selection of pollinator plants, both straight species and native cultivars. The nursery is operated organically with beneficial insects and natural, plant-based sprays.

Holland Ridge Farms

108 Rues Rd., Cream Ridge, NJ 08514
hollandridgefarms.com

AREA: 60 acres

HOURS: Open for festivals only, see website

ADMISSION: see website

AMENITIES:

EVENTS: Tulip Festival, Fall Flower Festival

There's nothing more beautiful in spring than acres of colorful tulips in bloom. You don't need to travel to Holland to see this sight, however. Holland Ridge Farms has been bringing a bit of Holland to southern New Jersey, and thousands of visitors flock to this annual event.

Casey Jansen Sr. purchased the 200-year-old dairy farm in 2018. Jansen comes from five generations of tulip growers in Holland and remembers picking tulips as a boy in his clogs. He came to New Jersey in the 1960s and spent 40 years growing tulips hydroponically in a greenhouse. When the farm came up for sale, Jansen jumped at the opportunity to expand his business and bring a bit of Holland to the area. The first tulip festival was launched that year to resounding success and has grown in size since then.

Today, the Jansens plant more than eight million tulips every year on 60 acres of farmland. To provide a dazzling display and ensure the most robust tulips, new bulbs are ordered every year from renowned suppliers in Holland. You will find tulips in every hue, from yellow to orange, pink, red, purple, and white as well as striated and marbled varieties. The "you-pick" tulip season lasts for two to three weeks in April. Visitors can pick their own bouquet of tulips then bring it to the bouquet wrapping station to have it packaged. Those who cannot attend in person can order Tulip Surprise Boxes with 20 stems of assorted colors that can be shipped anywhere in the country. Once the tulip season is over, thousands of summer flowers are planted in the fields in preparation for the Fall Flower Festival. In September you can pick sunflowers, dahlias, asters, gladiolus, callas, cosmos, zinnias, and many other flowers to create your own colorful bouquet.

The Jansens see their farm as a "theme park for flowers." The Tulip and Fall Flower festivals have evolved into all-day celebrations with hayrides, petting zoos, a bakery, and 30 food trucks. A gift shop features Dutch souvenirs. Since visitors also love to take photos, the Jansens have created more than 20 fun photo props including vintage barn doors, flower walls, a porch swing, a giant Dutch clog, bicycles, and a Cinderella-like carriage. The farm has become the site of many milestone events such as engagements, wedding ceremonies, baby showers, and parties.

PENNSYLVANIA

Suggested Daily Itineraries

Ambler Arboretum, Ambler (19)
Lunch–Magerk's Pub, Fort Washington
Highlands Mansion & Garden,
Fort Washington (17)

PHS Meadowbrook Farm,
Jenkintown (16)
Lunch–Drake Tavern, Jenkintown
Bowman's Hill Wildflower Preserve, New
Hope (3)
Hortulus Farm Garden & Nursery,
Wrightstown (4)

Bartram's Garden, Philadelphia (6)
Lunch–White Dog Cafe, Philadelphia
Shofuso Japanese Garden,
Philadelphia (7)
Wyck, Philadelphia (11)

Scott Arboretum of Swarthmore College,
Swarthmore (26)
Lunch–Terrain, Glen Mills
Tyler Arboretum, Media (27)

Longwood Gardens, Kennett Square (29)
Lunch– Longwood Gardens Cafe

Stoneleigh: A Natural Garden,
Villanova (20)
Lunch–Minella's Diner, Wayne
Chanticleer, Wayne (23)
Tea–A Taste of Britain, Wayne
Valley Forge Flowers, Wayne (23)

Morris Arboretum & Gardens,
Philadelphia (13)
Lunch–Morris Arboretum Cafe
The Barnes Arboretum at St. Joseph's
University, Merion (15)
Laurel Hill West, Bala Cynwyd (14)

23 **27** **29**

PENNSYLVANIA

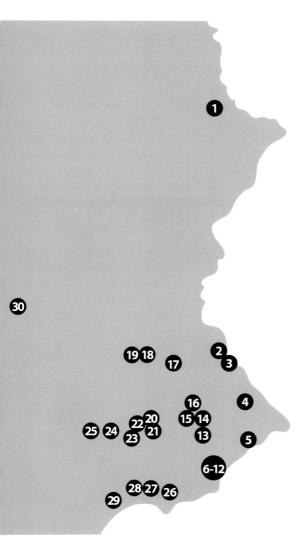

Grey Towers National Historic Site

122 Old Owego Turnpike, Milford, PA 18337
570-296-9630
fs.usda.gov/greytowers

AREA: 102 acres

HOURS: Grounds: daily dawn to dusk; mansion: Memorial Day–Oct.: Thurs.–Mon. 11–4

ADMISSION: $10

AMENITIES: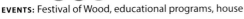

EVENTS: Festival of Wood, educational programs, house tours

Grey Towers was the home of the Pinchot family, prominent in business, politics, philanthropy, and forestry. It was originally built as a summer home in 1886 by James W. Pinchot. The design of the imposing 43-room mansion was based on LaGrange, the medieval French chateau of the Marquis de Lafayette. Named after its three massive towers, the mansion was constructed from local stone and timber by resident craftsmen and laborers.

When Grey Towers was built, nearly all the once-forested land surrounding it had been cleared for farming. While most of the country considered lumber an inexhaustible natural resource, James was disturbed by the destructive logging practices of his day. He cofounded the American Forestry Association, endowed the fledgling forestry program at Yale University, and

built a summer field camp at Grey Towers that trained professional foresters from 1901 to 1926.

His son Gifford became one of America's leading environmental conservation advocates at the turn of the century. Under President Teddy Roosevelt, he was named the chief of the U.S. Forest Service and helped to create more than 110 national forests across the country. His public service extended to two terms as governor of Pennsylvania.

Gifford and his wife, Cornelia, moved to Grey Towers in 1914. When you visit the property, you will be struck by its magnificent trees, particularly the copper beeches that Gifford planted in 1920. An allée of black locusts welcomes visitors to the estate. Hemlocks, confirmed by Governor Pinchot as Pennsylvania's state tree, form hedges throughout the garden. Lindens, aspens, black gums, maples, dogwoods, oaks, pines, and shagbark hickories surround the mansion.

Cornelia enjoyed gardening and entertaining and created the outbuildings and garden features that you see today. She engaged architect Chester Holmes Aldrich to add a water-filled half-moat in front of the mansion. Backed by a stone wall, the moat creates the look of a grand raised foundation. The Letter Box, a stone one-story cottage, was built as an office for political staff and an archive for Gifford's papers. The ornate Bait Box began as a playhouse and later served as Cornelia's tea room. Named for the family's love of fishing, it provided a quiet respite from the hustle and bustle of the main house. The Bait Box's stone entry was enclosed by stone walls with elliptical windows that frame views of the surrounding landscape. Cornelia's Long Garden with its rill, hemlock hedges, and perennial border, draws the eye to the Bait Box and creates a natural hallway between the two outdoor structures. Above the Long Garden is a swimming pool enclosed by a grape-covered pergola, flower beds, and a corner gazebo.

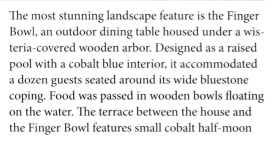

The most stunning landscape feature is the Finger Bowl, an outdoor dining table housed under a wisteria-covered wooden arbor. Designed as a raised pool with a cobalt blue interior, it accommodated a dozen guests seated around its wide bluestone coping. Food was passed in wooden bowls floating on the water. The terrace between the house and the Finger Bowl features small cobalt half-moon pools set in mosaic-inlaid paving. Two large terra-cotta urns and a shade garden frame the dining arbor.

In 1963 Dr. Gifford Bryce Pinchot, Gifford and Cornelia's son, donated Grey Towers and 102 acres to the U.S. Forest Service to carry forward the principles set forth by his father and grandfather.

The Gardens at Mill Fleurs

27 Cafferty Rd., Point Pleasant, PA 18950
215-297-1000
thegardensatmillfleurs.com

AREA: 5 acres

HOURS: April–Sept. : tours on select Saturdays, 10:30 am. See website.

ADMISSION: $25, reservations required

AMENITIES:

The Gardens at Mill Fleurs zigzag down a steep hillside to Tohickon Creek where two mills comprise the home and offices of furniture designers Barbara and Robert ("Tiff") Tiffany. The grist mill with its original millworks and water raceways dates from 1742, and the adjacent saw mill is from the 1790s. The name Mill Fleurs is a play on words and triple entendre, referring to the two mills; the French term for "a thousand flowers"; and the term for a historic glass-blowing technique with clusters of tiny glass flowers.

When the Tiffanys first bought the property in 1993, 10 acres of dangerous rock cliff and floodplain surrounded the historic but derelict buildings. After removing acres of rampant bamboo, multiflora rose, and poison ivy "trees," they began to plant the garden. The property was densely shaded by mature trees so woodland plants were required. Barbara has an intense curiosity about the natural world and was immediately drawn

to funky, weird, and interesting plants. Foliage shape, color, and plant form were more important to her than flowers. Today, the grounds feature more than 2,000 perennials, approximately 1,400 different varieties of woody plants, and 2,500 hosta cultivars—among many other specimens. You will see native and Asian plants like snowdrops, Solomon's seals, tricyrtis, astilbes, epimediums, rhododendrons, and hostas. Trees and shrubs are collected for variegated or colorful foliage and interesting bark. Plants with green, purple, or black flowers are favorites.

Densely planted borders supported by stone retaining walls line the walkways through the gardens. The garden is primarily organized by color or plant form. A sunny yellow garden with gold conifers, deutzias, and a stunning yellow magnolia and tree peony greets you at the entrance to the property. The driveway is planted in pink, with mature rhododendrons and dogwoods. The white garden sports plants with white flowers, variegated foliage, and trees with white bark, while other beds are planted in green, apricot, lavender, and purple. Patriot Hill is fabulous in April with masses of bluebells, red tulips, and white flowers. Adjacent to the house is the bronze-themed tropical garden displaying exotic plants like bananas, ti plants, and cordylines that are overwintered indoors. A vertical stone cliff is home to burgundy Japanese maples. A pinetum, dwarf conifer bed, and aesculus allée are just some of the landscape features dedicated to Barbara's plant collections. Beautiful benches designed by Robert offer spots to enjoy the views and fun pieces of old mill machinery enhance the borders.

Barbara loves to share her garden with visitors, and her guided tour with homemade refreshments lasts about two hours. Allow time to visit Tiffany Perennials where you will find rare and unusual plants for sale.

Bowman's Hill Wildflower Preserve

1635 River Rd., New Hope, PA 18938
215-862-2924
bhwp.org

AREA: 134 acres

HOURS: April–June: daily 9–5; July–March: Wed.–Mon. 9–5

ADMISSION: $12

AMENITIES:

EVENTS: Many workshops and educational programs

Bowman's Hill Wildflower Preserve is a living museum specifically devoted to native plants. With a variety of diverse habitats, from mature hardwood forests to meadows, ponds, creeks, and steep hillsides, the preserve is home to more than 700 of Pennsylvania's 2,000 native plants. These plants grow naturally in interdependent communities with resident insects, frogs, birds, and other wildlife.

Thanks to the efforts of two early conservationists—Mary K. Parry, chairman of the Bucks County Federation of Women's Clubs, and W. Wilson Heinitsh, a consultant for Washington Crossing Historic Park—100 acres were set aside in 1934 as a memorial to George Washington's encampment and a sanctuary for native plants. In the 1940s, under the leadership of Edgar T. Wherry, botany professor at the University of Pennsylvania, hundreds of native trees, shrubs, and wildflowers were planted on the site. His meticulous plant records set the stage for the preserve to become a horticultural institution.

Today, Bowman's Hill offers 4.5 miles of trails winding through forests and meadows. The woodlands are spectacular in spring, when large swaths of ephemerals burst into bloom. Spring ephemerals are native wildflowers that blossom before the trees leaf out, set seed, and often disappear completely underground during the summer months. In April you will find a sea of Virginia bluebells, carpets of trilliums, hepaticas, bloodroot, and Dutchman's breeches, followed by mayapples, twinleaf, and crested iris. The ponds and streams are fringed with bright yellow marsh marigolds. With the spring blooms of redbuds, dogwoods, fringe trees, and azaleas, the effect is magical. In the summer mountain laurels, swamp azaleas, and rosebay rhododendrons bloom in the woodlands, while bee balms, milkweeds, coneflowers, and penstemons fill the meadows with their colorful flowers. Fall brings out asters and goldenrods and brilliant foliage in shades of gold, orange, and red.

Bowman's Hill is also a haven for birdwatchers.

bygone days. On the other side of the wall is the Peony Walk with plants collected by Letitia in the early 1900s.

Surrounding the gardens, the Woodland Walk leads through an arboretum of more than 800 trees, shade gardens, and drifts of daffodils. Specimens of copper beech, cedar of Lebanon, lacebark pine, and Persian ironwood provide interest with their stature, colorful foliage, and mottled bark. In the spring witch hazels burst into bloom, followed by cherries, dogwoods, silverbells, fringe trees, snowbells, and stewartias. Andalusia's gardens and arboretum continue to evolve just as they have over the past 200 years, providing beauty and inspiration for all who visit.

Bartram's Garden

5400 Lindbergh Blvd., Philadelphia, PA 19143
215-729-5281
bartramsgarden.org

AREA: 50 acres

HOURS: Grounds: daily dawn–dusk; house: see website

ADMISSION: Free

AMENITIES: 🚻 ♿

EVENTS: Guided tours, plant sales, bike trails, fishing dock

John Bartram was America's first botanist, plant explorer, and collector. He compiled a stunning selection of flora at his home garden and nursery from plant collecting expeditions across eastern America, as well as through his trades with European collectors. Located on the west bank of the Schuylkill River, Bartram's Garden covers 50 acres. It includes his 1728 home and the historic botanical garden and arboretum that showcases North American plant species collected by three generations of Bartrams.

Bartram was a Quaker, a denomination that produced many naturalists at that time. He taught himself about plants through books and his own observations. His curiosity fueled a desire to collect plants from all over the East coast, as far south as Florida, and west to Lake Ontario. He collected seeds and plant specimens and established a relationship with another plant collector—London merchant Peter Collinson. Their plant swaps led

George Washington visiting Bartram

to a burgeoning business. Prominent patrons and scholars in Britain were fascinated by the native American species, and were eager to purchase from Bartram's Garden. In 1765 King George III appointed Bartram Royal Botanist. At home in Philadelphia, Bartram received both George Washington and Thomas Jefferson who shared a keen interest in horticulture.

Bartram's international plant trade and nursery business thrived under his descendants. Son William accompanied his father on most of his expeditions and became an important naturalist, author, and artist. William transformed the garden into an educational center that trained a new generation of botanists and explorers. Granddaughter Ann Bartram Carr built a successful nursery business that introduced Asian plants to the American public.

The Bartram garden has many distinct areas to explore. In front of the house is the Ann Bartram Carr garden, which celebrates her Asian plant introductions such as peonies and dahlias. Behind the house are the kitchen, flower, and medicinal gardens. And beyond those are woodlands of trees and shrubs that were collected, grown, and studied by the Bartrams from 1728 to 1850. These are primarily native plants of eastern North America: flame azaleas, highbush cranberry, Carolina allspice, sweetbay magnolia, and more. A bog garden illustrates the Bartrams' fascination with carnivorous plants. A separate area is devoted to plants William collected in the South, including bottlebrush buckeye and oakleaf hydrangea.

The garden also contains three especially notable trees:

Franklinia alatamaha: John and William Bartram discovered a small grove of these trees in October 1765 while camping by Georgia's Altamaha River. William eventually brought seeds home to

Philadelphia, where they were planted in 1777. The species, named in honor of their friend Benjamin Franklin, was last seen in the wild in 1803. All *Franklinia* growing today are descended from those propagated and distributed by the Bartrams, who saved this tree from extinction.

Cladrastis kentukia (Yellowwood): A notably old tree, possibly collected by French plant explorer Andre Michaux in Tennessee and sent to William in 1796.

Ginkgo biloba: The Bartrams' tree is believed to be one of three original ginkgos introduced to the United States from China in 1785.

The property continues to the edge of the river, where there are opportunities for water recreation. Native plants and those discovered by the Bartram family are available for purchase year-round in the Welcome Center.

Shofuso Japanese House and Garden

West Fairmount Park
Lansdowne Dr. & Horticultural Dr., Philadelphia, PA 19131
215-878-5097, japanphilly.org

AREA: 1.2 acres
HOURS: Late March–Oct.: Wed.–Sun. 11–5 ; Nov.–early
Dec.: Sat.–Sun. 10–5
ADMISSION: $14 by timed ticket
EVENTS: Cherry Blossom Festival, monthly tea ceremony,
cultural programs

Shofuso (Japanese for *Pine Breeze Villa*), is a traditional 17th century Japanese house and garden located in Philadelphia's Fairmount Park. It is part of the Japan America Society of Greater Philadelphia, which was formed to inspire a mutual understanding through art, business and culture. This site has been the home of several previous Japanese structures and gardens, dating back to the 1876 Centennial Exposition.

Shofuso originated as a special exhibition entitled "House in the Garden" in the courtyard of the Museum of Modern Art in New York City. It was designed and built in Nagoya, Japan, using traditional techniques and materials, including Hinoki cypress wood. It was disassembled and brought to New York, where it was rebuilt and exhibited for two years, to rave reviews. Shofuso's garden at MoMA was designed by Tansai Sano, a Kyoto landscape architect whose family were caretakers of the famous dry garden in the Ryoan-ji tem-

ple for six generations. Eighty main stones were shipped from the old temple's garden in central Japan to the exhibition in New York.

When the house and garden were relocated to Philadelphia in 1958, they were situated in a Japanese garden that had existed since 1909. A waterfall and a new planting scheme were added. The property was restored by a cadre of Japanese artisans in 1976, in preparation for the American Bicentennial celebration.

Three traditional types of Japanese gardens compose the 1.2-acre site: a hill-and-pond style garden which is intended to be viewed from the veranda; a *tsubo-niwa*, or courtyard garden, in the style of an urban 17th century Kyoto garden; and a *roji*, or tea garden, which is a rustic path to the tea house. In 2016 the *Journal of Japanese Gardening* ranked Shofuso third among 300 Japanese gardens in North America.

A majestic weeping cherry overlooks the house and pond. Cherry blossoms provide color in April, azaleas in May, the colorful leaves of Japanese maples in the fall, Visitors will enjoy the relaxing by the pond and feeding the giant koi year-round.

Center City Philadelphia Gardens

various locations

18th Century Garden

LOCATION: Walnut Street, between 3rd and 4th Streets

HOURS: Daily 9–dusk except major federal holidays

ADMISSION: Free

Defined by its lovely gazebo and grapevine-covered pergola, the 18th Century Garden illustrates the formal parterre gardens that were popular in Colonial times.

Rose Garden

LOCATION: Walnut Street and Locust Street, between 4th and 5th Streets

HOURS: Daily 9–dusk except major federal holidays

ADMISSION: Free

The Rose Garden displays 96 varieties of antique roses in shades of pink, red, white and coral. Since antique roses only bloom in late spring, they are augmented with modern hybrids to provide a longer season of color. A patch of cobblestone paving from the 19th century illustrates the original style of Philadelphia streets.

Magnolia Garden

LOCATION: Locust Street, between 4th and 5th Streets

HOURS: Daily 9–dusk except major federal holidays

ADMISSION: Free

This charming garden bursts into bloom in early spring with saucer magnolias, azaleas and daffodils. Thirteen magnolia trees line the garden's perimeter, representing the thirteen original colonies.

Benjamin Rush Garden

LOCATION: Corner of 3rd and Walnut Streets

HOURS: Daily 9–dusk except major federal holidays

ADMISSION: Free

A restful green oasis on the site of Benjamin Rush's home, this classic 18th century style garden features symmetrical planting beds bordered by low boxwood hedges. Hollies, groundcovers and seasonal annuals provide color year-round. The garden is being redesigned to showcase the Bicentennial Bell.

Thomas Jefferson Garden

LOCATION: American Philosophical Society, 104 S. 5th St.

HOURS: Daily 9–dusk

ADMISSION: Free

Dedicated to Thomas Jefferson who was an ardent horticulturist, this garden features roses, daylilies, salvias, hydrangeas, hollies, clematis, and other ornamentals encircling a formal lawn.

Hill-Physick House

321 S. 4th St., Philadelphia, PA 19106
215-925-7866
philalandmarks.org/hillphysick

AREA: .5 acre

HOURS: April–Nov.: Thurs.–Sat. 11–3, Sun. 12–3

ADMISSION: $10

AMENITIES:

EVENTS: Various special events

Built in 1786 by Henry Hill, a prominent patriot and wine merchant, this Federal house is the only free-standing mansion remaining in the colonial center of Philadelphia. As a tremendously successful merchant, Hill built an impressive home that reflected his social standing. The elegant three-story brick house was an exceptional example of the Federal style with an intricate fanlight imported from England crowning the double entry doors. The interior was designed for entertaining, with 32 rooms including a ballroom, spacious bedrooms, and mirrored fireplaces made with Valley Forge marble.

Dr. Philip Syng Physick acquired the house in 1815. The interior restoration interprets the grand Neoclassical style fashionable in his day, including beautiful French Zuber wallpaper and Federal and Empire style furnishings. Dr. Physick came from a prominent Quaker Philadelphia family. Known today and in his own time as the "Father of American Surgery," Dr. Physick trained in London and Edinburgh before setting up his practice in Philadelphia. He saw patients at his home and also performed surgeries in the homes of his well-to-do patients, which included Dolley Madison, Andrew Jackson, and Chief Justice John Marshall. He taught surgery and anatomy at the University of Pennsylvania, training an entire generation of doctors in his innovative surgical techniques. He designed many medical instruments, some of which are still in use today, such as the stomach pump, catgut sutures, and rubber band ligatures. Exhibits of Dr. Physick's surgical tools are found on the second floor of the mansion and include bloodletting instruments, stomach pumps, clamps, and tubes used to remove kidney stones.

After Dr. Physick's death in 1837, his descendants lived in the house until the mid-20th century, when the house was acquired by the Pennsylvania Hospital. In the late 1960s, publisher Walter Annenberg restored the house and donated it to the Philadelphia Society for the Preservation of Landmarks to be opened to the public as a house museum.

Enclosed by a brick wall draped with wisteria, the garden surrounding the Hill-Physick House is a quiet retreat in the midst of a bustling city. Stately sycamores and maples provide shade during Philadelphia's hot summer months. A winding brick walkway encircles a lawn bordered with beds of camellias and dogwoods underplanted with shade-loving shrubs and perennials. In the spring azaleas and rhododendrons burst into bloom, followed by oakleaf and panicle hydrangeas in summer. Hostas, anemones, ferns, and ivies create a tapestry of foliage and flowers.

The Mütter Museum at The College of Physicians of Philadelphia

19 S. 22nd St., Philadelphia, PA 19103
215-563-3737
muttermuseum.org

AREA: .5 acre
HOURS: Wed.–Mon. 10–5
ADMISSION: $20
AMENITIES:
EVENTS: Exhibitions, literary seminars, concerts

The Mütter Museum is regarded as the finest museum of medical history in the nation. Located in a grand 100-year-old building in the city center, the museum displays beautifully preserved collections of medical instruments, anatomical specimens, and models in original 19th century display cases.

The museum began as a donation to The College of Physicians of Philadelphia by Dr. Thomas Dent Mütter (1811-1859), a renowned surgeon and fellow of the college. Dr. Mütter's goal was to improve and reform medical education. His gift of 1,700 objects and $30,000 included stipulations for the maintenance and growth of the collection as well as the funding of annual lectures. Since the museum's inception, the collection has grown to more than 25,000 objects. A robust education program introduces middle and high school students to the history and culture of medicine, as well as careers in healthcare and biosciences.

The College of Physicians of Philadelphia has a long history dating back to 1787. One of its founders was Benjamin Rush, a Philadelphia doctor, civic leader, and signer of the Declaration of Independence. At that time, the study of botany was a crucial component of a doctor's medical education. Rush urged the college fellows to create a medicinal garden that would encourage the study of healing plants and provide a supply of these plants to doctors and students.

The Benjamin Rush Medicinal Plant Garden was finally installed in 1937 to commemorate the college's 150th anniversary. Set in an enclosed courtyard adjacent to the Mütter Museum, the garden displays more than 60 different kinds of herbs that have both historical and contemporary medicinal value. The courtyard is formal in design with herringbone brick pathways and a bluestone patio. Four beds densely planted with medicinal

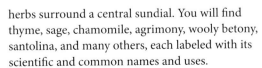

herbs surround a central sundial. You will find thyme, sage, chamomile, agrimony, wooly betony, santolina, and many others, each labeled with its scientific and common names and uses.

In 2019 the garden was refreshed with new plantings. Columnar sweet gums 'Slender Silhouette' are planted to soften a tall brick wall. A White Garden was added, inspired by Vita Sackville-West's iconic garden at Sissinghurst. Bright white anemones, hydrangeas, and feverfew are augmented with the silver foliage of lavender, dusty miller, and silver cypresses in metal planters. Benches in the shade of a sweetbay magnolia offer museum visitors a pleasant spot to relax and enjoy the garden.

Wyck

6026 Germantown Ave., Philadelphia, PA 19144
215-848-1690
wyck.org

AREA: 2.5 acres
HOURS: April–Nov.: Thurs.–Sat. 12–4
ADMISSION: Free
AMENITIES: 🏛 👪 ♿
EVENTS: Rose Tours in May and June, Honey Festival in Sept. and many more programs

Wyck is a haven for both history buffs and gardeners. As the ancestral home of the Wistar/Haines family for nine generations from 1690 to 1973, it illustrates the remarkable survival of historic Philadelphia life in a densely populated urban neighborhood. The 2.5-acre site includes a beautiful rose garden, perennial gardens, a woodlot, fruit trees, and vegetable and herb gardens. The Colonial house is surrounded by a carriage house, greenhouse, icehouse, and smokehouse, and features a collection of more than 10,000 family objects, furniture, and historical curiosities.

Wyck's owners were Quakers, committed to innovation, social responsibility, and environmental sustainability. They became leaders in business, natural history, science, education reform, and horticulture. Reuben Haines III (1786–1831)

founded the Academy of Natural Sciences, the Franklin Institute, and the Pennsylvania Horticultural Society. Jane Bowne Haines II (1869–1937) was instrumental in the establishment of the Garden Club of America and founded the Pennsylvania School of Horticulture for Women, one of the first of such schools in the country (see Ambler Arboretum).

The gardens at Wyck have remained largely intact since the 1820s and contain heirloom plants that have disappeared from other historic gardens. The largest tree in the garden is a native tulip poplar from the 1830s. A horse chestnut replaced the original Spanish chestnuts, which were wiped out by the chestnut blight of the early 20th century. The small pawpaw grove descends from native pawpaws grown on the property for at least 100 years.

The famous Rose Garden has changed little since Jane Bowen Haines I designed it in the 1820s. It is the oldest rose garden in its original plan in America, with more than 50 cultivars planted in parterres. The intimate garden retains its old-world charm, enclosed on one side by a wisteria arbor and on the other by a romantic garden shelter. (Legend has it that wisteria is named after the Wistar family.) Wyck's historic roses are remarkable for their beauty as well as for their fragrance, which fills the garden in May and June.

Also at Wyck is the Home Farm, a half-acre garden with vegetables, annuals, perennials, and fruiting plants. A historic 1914 Lord & Burnham greenhouse is used for seed starting, and several beehives produce honey. Food grown on the farm is distributed to the community through the free Home Farm Club program.

Laurel Hill East

3822 Ridge Ave., Philadelphia, PA 19132
610-668-9900
laurelhillphl.com

AREA: West: 187 acres; East: 78 acres
HOURS: Spring–Fall: daily 7–7
ADMISSION: Free
EVENTS: Lectures, tours, workshops

Established in 1836, Laurel Hill East is the first National Historic Landmark Cemetery and the second garden-designed cemetery in the United States. At a time when city burial grounds were overcrowded and often unsanitary, the rural cemetery was a novel idea that predated public parks and arboretums. From its inception, Laurel Hill was intended as a multipurpose cultural attraction. Founder John Jay Smith envisioned the cemetery as a place where the general public could experience architecture, art, horticulture, and beautiful landscapes previously available only to the wealthy.

Scottish architect Jon Notman designed the cemetery as a series of terraces that descend to the Schuylkill River. Visitors entered the cemetery through a grand gatehouse with a massive Roman arch surrounded by an imposing classical colonnade. More than 2,400 trees were planted to frame beautiful views and create a verdant garden. Many were rare species from other parts of the world. Planted in groups or as single specimens, the copper beeches, hollies, magnolias, gingkos,

dogwoods, and Japanese maples created a beautiful display. They surrounded an astounding array of gravestones, mausoleums, obelisks, and monuments, many created by renowned sculptors. The cemetery rapidly became a popular destination for locals and tourists, who strolled, picnicked, and admired the trees and monuments. In 1861 the cemetery had more than 140,000 visitors tickets and were required for admission.

An interesting feature of the cemetery are the cradle graves that resemble a bed, with the gravestone as the headboard, a footstone, and two connecting low walls. Plantings of flowers create a colorful blanket. Cradle graves were popular in the Victorian era, especially for the graves of children. They were lovingly maintained by the families of the deceased.

The gardens at Laurel Hill continue to evolve. New pollinator gardens were installed in front of the entrance, with native perennials such as coneflower, coreopsis, scabiosa, salvia, and butterfly weed that provide a food source for birds, bees, and butterflies. The Old Mortality Rock Garden was redesigned with local Wissahickon schist and reclaimed architectural elements from the cemetery. Pink balloon flowers, shrub clematis, ice plants, and other unusual bulbs, ephemerals, and perennials thrive on its rocky slopes.

PENNSYLVANIA

Laurel Hill West

225 Belmont Ave., Bala Cynwyd, PA 19004
610-668-9900
laurelphl.com

AREA: 187 acres
HOURS: Spring–Fall: daily 7–7
ADMISSION: Free
EVENTS: Lectures, tours, workshops

The expansion of Fairmount Park in the 1860s prevented further growth of the original Laurel Hill cemetery (now Laurel Hill East.) In 1869 John Jay Smith established Laurel Hill West across the Schuylkill River in neighboring Lower Merion Township. The hilly property was enclosed on two sides by deep ravines, which ensured privacy and deterred nearby development. Like its sister across the river, Laurel Hill West was designed as a scenic landscape with panoramic views of the river and thousands of unusual trees. A greater emphasis was placed on sweeping lawns and wide vistas. Fencing of burial plots and other hedge barriers were discouraged to preserve wide open spaces. Where families were encouraged to plant their own burial properties in the older cemetery, Laurel Hill West directed the locations and varieties of plants that were incorporated in its landscape.

Some of the recently added garden areas at Laurel Hill West include the Chapel of Peace garden. This formal garden with climbing roses, perennials, and flowering planters complements the Gothic-style architecture of the historic chapel. Nature's Sanctuary is the new green burial area, which functions both as a natural burial site and native plant meadow. Flowering perennials, shrubs, and trees provide seasonal color and benefit native pollinators and other wildlife.

Today, both Laurel Hill East and West are accredited arboretums with more than 6,000 trees and shrubs representing 700 species and cultivars. The arboretums are especially beautiful in April and May when the flowering cherries, magnolias, and dogwoods burst into bloom, and then in autumn when the leaves turn to magnificent shades of gold, orange, and red. Some of the notable trees include American and cut-leaf lindens, English yews, Himalayan pines, weeping European beeches, maples, hemlocks, and weeping Japanese pagoda trees. With an arborist on staff, the trees are beautifully pruned to show off their unique forms.

Morris Arboretum & Gardens

University of Pennsylvania, 100 E. Northwestern Ave., Philadelphia, PA 19118
215-247-5777
morrisarboretum.org

AREA: 175 acres

HOURS: Mon.–Fri. 10–5, Sat.–Sun. 9–5

ADMISSION: $20

AMENITIES:

EVENTS: Moonlight & Roses, many courses, lectures, family programs, holiday railroad display

In 1887 brother and sister John and Lydia Morris purchased farmland in northern Philadelphia to build a summer home and garden. Children of a prominent Philadelphia Quaker family, the Morrises were keenly interested in travel, history, art, and botany. They also had a deep belief in the importance of community, education, land stewardship, and conservation. Compton, the estate that they founded in Chestnut Hill, eventually grew to more than 166 acres with the acquisition of neighboring farms. Through perseverance and hard work, the once-barren property was transformed into a lush botanic garden.

John was a knowledgeable plantsman and collector. He and Lydia traveled extensively in Asia, Europe, and America, collecting native and exotic plants, sculptures, and design ideas from the gardens that they visited. Through friendships and

acquisitions from horticulturists throughout the world, including plant hunter E. H. Wilson, they assembled a collection of 3,500 plant cultivars.

Over 30 years the Morrises developed an eclectic garden inspired by those they had visited—a blend of picturesque English landscape with formal European and Asian elements. Many of the Morrises' unique structures are still part of the garden today: a Victorian-style greenhouse called a fernery; a log cabin in the woodland that served as Lydia's private retreat; and the Mercury Loggia, which commemorated the 25th anniversary of the Compton estate. The loggia is a temple-like stone structure with a bronze statue of Mercury and a grotto overlooking the Ravine Garden. A trip to the Alhambra inspired the Long Fountain with its arching water jets while Italian villa gardens served as the model for the Orange Balustrade garden with its rock waterfall, hillside location, steps, and balustrade.

There are many plant collections and themed areas throughout the arboretum that provide interest in all four seasons. Created in 1888, the walled Rose Garden is one of the loveliest and oldest features of the Morris estate. Once a traditional rose collection, the garden has been updated with a mix of roses, perennials, and shrubs for a lush display. The Alice & J. Liddon Pennock Flower Walk honors Liddon Pennock (see PHS Meadowbrook Farm). Designed as both a teaching garden and a vibrant ornamental garden, it is planted in brilliant hues of orange, red, chartreuse, and purple. The historic Rock Wall Garden is home to creeping and cascading plants such as sedums, campanulas, and thymes that grow in its crevices. The English Park displays a collection of exotic trees and shrubs from Asia, including magnolias and azaleas. The arboretum's living collection of 11,000 plants comprises many rare trees and specimens.

PHS Meadowbrook Farm

1633 Washington Ln., Meadowbrook, PA 19046
215-887-5900
phsonline.org/locations/phs-meadowbrook-farm

AREA: 21 acres, 2 acres of gardens

HOURS: Mid-April–mid-Oct.: Wed. & Fri. 10–4,
Thurs. & Sat.: 10–6

ADMISSION: Free

AMENITIES:

EVENTS: House tours, workshops

PHS Meadowbrook Farm is a beautiful public garden located just outside of Philadelphia. It is the legacy of the late J. Liddon Pennock, Jr., a longtime prominent figure in the Delaware Valley's floral and horticultural design world.

Pennock came from a long line of florists, the first of whom arrived in Philadelphia in 1688 to garden on a land grant of a few thousand acres. Pennock took over the family business at age 20 and became florist to the Philadelphia elite, creating bouquets for society weddings and centerpieces for debutante balls. Most notably he was appoint-

ed as the White House's floral director during the Nixon administration, decorating it for holidays, state visits, and Tricia Nixon's wedding. Pennock also served as director of the Philadelphia Flower Show and president of the Pennsylvania Horticultural Society.

Situated on 21 acres, Meadowbrook Farm was Pennock's home for 58 years. The two-story English Cotwolds-style house sits atop a hill, capturing dramatic views. The interior is exquisitely decorated and sometimes open for touring. Pennock created 15 intimate garden rooms on his terraced property. Many feature a fountain, statuary, pool, or gazebo from a past flower show, and most have a place to sit and enjoy the view. No more than 30 feet wide, the garden rooms are enclosed by stone walls or hedges. They intersect to create allées that stretch hundreds of feet, creating the illusion of

great space in just two acres of formal gardens. Each boasts a memorable name, such as the Eagle Garden, Dipping Pool, Lyre Garden, or Franklinia Walk. Each garden room has a formal structure with plantings that are rich in detail and combine traditional and contemporary styles. You will find collections of rhododendrons, specimen trees, unusual shrubs, perennials and vines, accented with tropicals and annuals for seasonal color. Mixed containers, statues, and unique architectural details decorate each area. Horticultural specimens are cleverly shaped, such as the espaliered magnolia on the back patio, or the yew in the front courtyard that is pruned into a cloud formation.

The lizard figurines throughout the garden are a reminder of Pennock, whose nickname was "Lizard" (a corruption of Liddon.)

After retiring from the floral business in the early 1970s, Pennock opened a retail greenhouse specializing in tropicals and topiaries. When he passed away in 2003, he bequeathed Meadowbrook Farm to the Pennsylvania Horticultural Society, which has opened the property to the public.

The Barnes Arboretum at St. Joseph's University

50 Lapsley Ln., Merion, PA 19066
610-660-2802
sju.edu/barnesarboretum

AREA: 12 acres

HOURS: Mon.–Fri. 8:30–5:30, Sat.–Sun. 11–5:30 except university holidays

ADMISSION: Free, donations appreciated

AMENITIES: 👫

EVENTS: Classes and workshops

The Barnes Arboretum at St. Joseph's University began as a collection of 200 specimen trees assembled by Civil War veteran Captain Joseph Lapsley Wilson in the 1880s. The 12-acre property was purchased in 1922 by Dr. Albert C. Barnes and his wife, Laura Leggett Barnes. They hired renowned French architect Paul Cret to design a gallery and residence on the grounds. Albert was a collector of Impressionist and early Modernist paintings as well as sculpture and decorative arts. Laura was an avid horticulturist. This estate became the first home of the Barnes Foundation, an educational institution dedicated to promoting an appreciation of fine art and horticulture.

Laura Barnes' legacy lives on in the beauty of the landscape, the teaching collections of the arboretum and in the horticulture school that she founded in 1940. As director of the arboretum for 40 years, Laura corresponded and exchanged specimens with many other botanic gardens, including the Arnold Arboretum and the Brooklyn Botanic Garden. Despite its small size, the Barnes is home to over 3,000 varieties of woody plants, including 30 Pennsylvania Champion Trees. Some of the remarkable tree specimens include the Chinese pistache, giant sequoia, Japanese umbrella pine, Persian ironwood, Sakhalin cork tree, and monkey puzzle tree.

The landscape was designed with formal gardens of roses and perennials, a series of plant collections, and an arboretum on the periphery. The rose garden includes the fragrant 'Auguste Renoir' hybrid with its old-fashioned, full, rounded blooms—a nod to the many Renoir

paintings in the Barnes collection. The historic herbaceous garden was recenly redesigned for pollinator support and year-round interest, and exhibits beautiful flower combinations. From the formal gardens, walking paths meander around a meadow fringed with rare trees, a pond with a tea house, and through educational collections of trees and shrubs. Laura designed the garden for four-season interest, and included trees with beautiful exfoliating bark such as stewartia, lacebark pine, and Japanese clethra that can take center stage during the winter months. Since the arboretum is a teaching garden, it was laid out as a synoptic collection, where similar plants were grouped together so horticulture students could learn by comparison. It features mature collections of aesculus, clethra, magnolia, lilac, peony, and viburnum. Dating back to the early 1900s, these plants are important genetic resources for conservation and study. There are also large collections of ornamental ferns and hostas in the shady woodlands. Adjacent to the visitor center you will find a medicinal garden with plants arranged according to the healing systems in which they are used, in allopathic medicine, homeopathy, aromatherapy, and traditional Chinese and Native American medicine. The Arboretum's herbarium of 10,000 preserved specimens is a valuable resource for students and scholars.

After the Barnes art collection moved to Center City in Philadelphia in 2012, the Barnes Foundation and St. Joseph's University launched an educational collaboration that will lead to an expansion of the Horticulture Certificate Program. The restored gallery building now houses St. Joseph's art museum with its collection of Latin American Colonial art, stained glass windows, and plaster casts. Some of the interior furnishings were made from the Arboretum's decaying Chinese toon trees (*Toona sinensis*), which grow to 65 feet in height and produce pendulous clusters of small flowers.

Highlands Mansion and Gardens

7001 Sheaff Ln., Fort Washington, PA 19034
215-641-2687
highlandshistorical.org

AREA: 44 acres, 2 acre garden
HOURS: Gardens: Tues.–Sun. dawn–dusk
ADMISSION: $5
AMENITIES:
EVENTS: Mansion & garden tours on weekdays at 1:30

Highlands Mansion and Gardens was home to three families during its 300-year history. The original owner was Anthony Morris, a wealthy politician and merchant who purchased 200 acres in Whitemarsh, Montgomery County in 1794. There he constructed an elaborate country estate named The Highlands to shelter his family from the yellow fever epidemics sweeping Philadelphia. Morris suffered extreme financial difficulties and in 1808 was forced to sell The Highlands.

Philadelphia wine merchant George Sheaff bought the property in 1813, and his descendants owned it for more than a century. They created the two-acre "pleasure" garden east of the house, with its crenelated stone walls, formal perennial borders, grapery, and gardener's cottage. The noted 19th century architect and critic Andrew Jackson Downing described the garden as "one of the most remarkable in Pennsylvania," and in 1844 praised

The Highlands as "a striking example of science, skill, and taste applied to a country seat," noting that "there are few in the Union, taken as a whole, superior to it."

In 1917 socialite Caroline Sinkler, a native South Carolinian with ties to Philadelphia, purchased The Highlands and began extensive renovations to both the mansion and gardens. She created the current two-acre formal Colonial Revival garden, which earned a medal of excellence in 1933 from the Pennsylvania Horticultural Society. She also added stone walls, the exedra, and the greenhouse.

Walking through The Highlands can feel like a trip to Scotland. Long herbaceous borders culminate in a central fountain. A rose-covered pergola leads to boxwood-edged flower beds. Statuary and urns punctuate the landscape. An elegant herb parterre complements a Gothic Revival gardener's house. The aged stone walls are draped in grape ivy. Look for the ha-ha in front of the mansion, which was once used to keep farm animals in their pasture, and the exedra, which shapes a secret garden room.

Beyond the gardens, you can explore nine picturesque outbuildings, including a barn, springhouse, greenhouse, smokehouse, ice house, and tool shed. The Highlands Historical Society now owns the property, and has worked hard to restore the buildings and gardens to their historical beauty.

Ambler Arboretum of Temple University

580 Meetinghouse Rd., Ambler, PA 19002
267-468-8000
ambler.temple.edu

AREA: 187 acre campus
HOURS: Daily dawn–dusk
ADMISSION: Free
AMENITIES:
EVENTS: Guided tours available, $5

The Ambler Arboretum of Temple University is a historic public garden that serves as a living laboratory for students of horticulture and environmental science. Its three areas of focus are sustainability, the health benefits of gardens, and the history of women in horticulture, agriculture, and design.

The Arboretum originated in 1910 with Jane Bowne Haines II, a descendant of the Wyck family of Germantown (see Wyck). A graduate of Bryn Mawr College, Haines had toured Europe, visiting several colleges of gardening in England and Germany. When she returned home, she was determined to create a similar institution in the United States. With financial support from friends and fellow Bryn Mawr alumnae, she purchased a 71-acre farm near Ambler, where she founded the Pennsylvania School of Horticulture for Women. A colonial farmhouse on the property was renovated to provide offices, staff space, a classroom,

and dining hall, and in 1911, the school welcomed its first five students.

In the early 1900s women had few choices beyond marriage and family life, and the idea of educating them for careers in horticulture and agriculture was radical. The school played a unique role in both women's history and garden history. As the decades passed, enrollment remained small, but students went on to successful careers at institutions such as Longwood Gardens, Brooklyn Botanic Garden, Morris Arboretum, Colonial Williamsburg, and the National Arboretum. In 1958 the school became part of Temple University.

You can take a self-guided tour of the 13 campus gardens, beginning with the Viola Anders Herb Garden, which displays a collection of culinary, dye, and medicinal herbs. The Arboretum's centerpiece is the Formal Perennial Garden, designed by Beatrix Farrand and Professor James Bush-Brown in 1928. In May the long borders are ablaze with peonies, giant alliums, and baptisia. Twin gazebos surrounding a circular pond serve both as vantage points and focal points when the garden is viewed from the stairs of Dixon Hall.

Other gardens include the naturalistic Woodland Garden, with its lovely collection of spring-blooming bulbs, shrubs and trees. The Ground Cover Garden displays perennials suited for mass plantings. The Winter Garden features trees and shrubs with colorful branches, textured bark, and berries, underplanted with early-flowering bulbs. A conifer collection borders the greenhouses. The Healing Garden is an oasis of calm and rejuvenation, designed around a central labyrinth. It features a rain garden that captures and purifies storm-water runoff. The Wetland Garden is an education in sustainable landscaping, with recycled-glass pavers, a biological filtration system for campus storm water runoff, a solar fountain, and plantings of natives.

Northview

Ambler, PA
beforeyougarden@gmail.com
jenneyrosecarey.com

AREA: 4.5 acres

HOURS: By appointment only

Jenny Rose Carey is a lifelong gardener, educator, author, garden historian, and self-proclaimed "hortnut." Born in England to a family of botanists, she grew up gardening, exploring meadows and woodlands, and visiting renowned estates such as Sissinghurst and Great Dixter. Jenny Rose has taught at Temple University and the Barnes Foundation, and served as director of the Ambler Arboretum of Temple University and PHS Meadowbrook Farm. Northview, her 4.5-acre garden in Ambler, served as the inspiration for two of her books, *Glorious Shade* (2017) and *The Ultimate Flower Gardener's Guide* (2022.)

Jenny Rose and her husband moved to their Victorian home Northview in 1997. The property was once a model farm created by Wilmer Atkinson, editor of *The Farm Journal* in the late 1800s, and featured Japanese maples and Scots pines from that era. By the time that Jenny Rose began gardening at Northview, it was overgrown with Norway maples, poison ivy, and many other invasives. Like her predecessors, Jenny Rose views herself as a steward of the land, making it better for future generations. After clearing the lot, Jenny

Rose planted the Herb Garden that is now the central hub of Northview. Herb growing had been a passion since childhood, and Jenny Rose filled the garden with culinary, medicinal, and dyeing herbs. A Woodland Garden followed, planted with bloodroot, Virginia bluebells, and other perennials shared by friends and family. It is now home to a Victorian-style Stumpery and a Moss Garden with a whimsical teapot fountain.

As Jenny Rose's plant collections grew, more garden rooms followed: the Winter Walk of 45 witch hazels, snowdrops, and sarcococcas; the Redbud Allée; the Spring Garden of crocuses, daffodils, grape hyacinths, and tulips; and a Pond Garden with moisture-loving plants. Garden room themes were often dictated by the cultivation requirements of certain plants. A trip to Provence inspired Jenny Rose to grow lavender, which resulted in a Dry Garden that is host to many other silver-leaved plants from the Mediterranean. A mounded rocky area around a second pond forms the Lake Garden and is home to tiny floral treasures tucked into its planting pockets. Other gardens, like the Fruit and Flower Garden, the Cutting Garden, and the Hugelkulturs, arose from their use or style of cultivation.

The garden is deeply intertwined with Jenny Rose's life as a mother, professor, author, lecturer, and photographer. Whether it is teaching her children about pollinators, college students about botany, garden club members about cultivation techniques, or providing readers with photos and advice about plant varieties, her garden offers endless opportunities to educate and inspire. Northview is a welcoming garden with plenty of seating areas that invite visitors to relax and enjoy the views. Even the "work areas" are beautifully designed with greenhouses, cold frames, charming summerhouses, and garden sheds that invite you to enjoy the rewarding work of gardening.

Stoneleigh, A Natural Garden

1829 East County Line Rd., Villanova, PA 19085
610-353-5587 x200
stoneleighgarden.org

AREA: 42 acres

HOURS: Tues.–Sun. 10–5

ADMISSION: Free

AMENITIES:

EVENTS: Many educational programs

Opened in 2018, Stoneleigh is one of the Philadelphia region's newest public gardens. With majestic trees, sweeping vistas, intimate garden spaces, and dynamic plantings of native plants, the historic property offers opportunities to explore, learn, relax, and be inspired.

Stoneleigh's history dates back to 1877 when railroad executive Edmund Smith purchased 65 acres of land in Villanova for a "gentleman's farm." In the early 1900s, second owner Samuel Bodine worked with the Olmsted Brothers firm to transform the landscape from Beaux Arts formality to a naturalistic parklike setting. Entrepreneur Otto Haas purchased the estate in 1932, launching an 80-year tenure of careful stewardship by the Haas family. Otto's son John and his wife, Chara, acquired the property in 1964 and lived there for the next five decades. The Haases favored a naturalistic approach to the landscape. Upon their death, Stoneleigh was donated to Natural Lands to preserve it in perpetuity.

Today, Stoneleigh is a historic estate with creative contemporary gardens that celebrate the natural world. Architectural elements from the early 20th century, such as the Circle Garden, Pergola, and Rockery, have been updated with a dynamic combinations of native plants. The 220-foot-long stone Pergola is draped in American wisteria and colorful honeysuckles. Catalpa Court, named for its massive 150-year-old catalpa tree, features a dramatic water garden with a cascading edge. Native aquatic plants provide chemical-free filtration and a safe habitat for birds and amphibians. The former in-ground pool area is now a flagstone patio inset with circular bog gardens of pitcher plants, sundews, and other natives. The original Olmsted Brothers Meadow Vista has been restored with native grasses and wildflowers that benefit pollinators and other wildlife.

The garden style at Stoneleigh, is "native with a twist." The twist may be an interesting variegated cultivar of a native plant, like the gold-speckled witch hazel 'Lemon Lime.' Or it may be an unusual use of a plant, like an espalier of redbud 'Black Pearl' on the wall of the mansion. Instead of a yew hedge, you will also find mixed hedges of evergreens, viburnums, hydrangeas, and hornbeams that change a monoculture into a diverse and environmentally friendly garden feature.

Stoneleigh is managed with sustainable practices that promote biodiversity and benefit the environment in many ways, from reducing chemical applications, controlling erosion, mitigating stormwater runoff, to reducing energy consumption in garden maintenance. More than 25,000 native plants have been added to the garden, creating habitats for insects, birds, and other wildlife. The combination of classical architecture and 21st-century gardening philosophy provides a unique botanical garden experience.

Chanticleer

786 Church Rd., Wayne, PA 19087
610-687-4163
chanticleergarden.org

AREA: 48 acres
HOURS: April–Oct. : Wed. –Sun. 10–5. May–Labor Day: Fri. till 8 pm
ADMISSION: $15
AMENITIES:
EVENTS: Lectures, workshops, classes

Chanticleer has been called the most romantic, imaginative, and exciting public garden in America. This innovative 30-year-old public garden is one of 25 gardens featured in Tim Richardson's *Great Gardens of America*, and was named one of the "Top 10 North American Gardens Worth Traveling For" by the North American Garden Tourism Conference. Artistic, bold, and breathtaking, it has remained true to its founder's vision of being a "pleasure garden" for visitors.

The Chanticleer estate dates from the early 20th century, when Philadelphians eager to escape the heat of the city built summer homes along the Main Line of the Pennsylvania Railroad. Adolph Rosengarten, whose pharmaceutical business became part of Merck, built his country retreat in 1913. His son Adolph Jr., began creating the

magnificent garden when he came home from World War II. He had been stationed in Bletchley Park in England and fell in love with English estate gardens. Adolph Jr. and his wife, Janet, both enjoyed gardening, and maintained a huge vegetable garden, as well as flowers, shrubs and trees. He received an award from the American Horticultural Society as "one of the foremost gardeners in the country." When he left the property to the public following his death in 1990, the charter stipulated: "Operate the property as a beautiful public garden.… Educate amateur and professional gardeners."

Staying true to its mission, Chanticleer has evolved into a horticultural triumph. While the original magnificent lawns, trees, historic buildings, and terraces remain, the staff added thematic garden rooms filled with creative plantings that are an inspiration to both professional and home gardeners.

The Teacup Garden is Chanticleer's courtyard—an intimate space anchored by a small Italianate fountain enclosed by a columned pergola. In the spring the fountain is surrounded by a lively combination of flowering bulbs, heucheras, grasses, and herbs. In summer and fall, tropicals, succulents, bananas, pineapple lilies, and dozens of exuberant planters fill the small garden to overflowing.

What was once the old tennis court has been transformed into a bold flower garden. Its serpentine beds feature architectural plants and those with strong textures and foliage color. Sculpted yew hedges frame the dazzling plantings.

The southwest-facing, sunbaked Gravel Garden is home to Mediterranean plants. In the spring this garden is graced with species tulips, miniature daffodils, and columbines. Come summer, orange butterfly weed, lavender, Mexican feather grass, thyme, and yuccas explode in a tapestry on the hillside.

Beyond the slope, Bell's Run is a quiet respite surrounded by woodlands carpeted with grape hyacinths, trilliums, and primroses. The undulating lawn along the stream is a vision in blue when thousands of camassias bloom in the spring.

Planted with hundreds of azaleas, foam flowers, and ferns, Bell's Woodland celebrates plants of the eastern North American forest. You enter through a bridge sculpted to resemble a giant fallen beech tree that spans the creek. Wetland plants including

skunk cabbage, rushes, and sedges line the creek bed, while spring ephemerals bloom under the deciduous trees.

The Ruin Garden, built on the site of Adolph's residence, is composed of three theatrical rooms: a Great Hall with a fountain resembling a large sarcophagus resting on a mosaic "rug" of tile, slate, and granite; a "Library" of books sculpted out of stone; and a "Pool Room," where haunting marble faces gaze up from the depths of a grave-like water feature.

Throughout Chanticleer you will find handcrafted benches, chairs, metal railings, and decorations—the creations of employees who contribute not only their horticultural skills but also their artistic talents of woodworking, stone carving, painting, and metalworking.

A favorite design element at Chanticleer are the decorative containers. Richly planted with unusual combinations, these pots are works of art. Every year and every season bring a fresh scheme. It's worth returning several times a year just to see what's new in the pots!

Carolyn's Shade Gardens

Bryn Mawr, PA 19010
carolynsshadegardens.com

AREA: 2 acres
HOURS: By appointment only
AMENITIES: 🏪
EVENTS: Sale days

Carolyn Walker writes an informative illustrated blog called *Carolyn's Shade Gardens: The Joys of Gardening in the Shadows* and sells a wonderful selection of perennials and bulbs that thrive in shade gardens.

One side of her property is dominated by large London plane trees that once lined an old carriage path. Beneath these graceful trees, Carolyn has created a woodland garden that is a living catalog of plants that are happy in the dappled shade. About 200 varieties of hostas, hellebores, pulmonarias, primroses, corydalis, hardy cyclamens, Virginia bluebells, winter aconites, and heucheras grow there and are available for sale.

Carolyn's gardens and production beds are maintained completely organically. She propagates and grows more than 50% of the plants that are available for sale without the use of fertilizers,

chemical sprays (except for deer), or supplemental watering. These are low-maintenance shade plants that thrive in woodland gardens. Carolyn's display beds allow you to see mature plants in a landscape setting, which is particularly valuable for hostas which often show their unique texture or variegation several years after planting.

A self-described "galanthophile," Carolyn provides one of the few sources of unusual snowdrops in the U.S. There are few other places where you can find snowdrops with yellow markings, crinkled double blooms, or pagoda-shaped flowers. These are unique, collectible varieties, available by mail-order only, and shipped in late winter. Together with hellebores, they are the stars of the winter garden. The shade perennials are available for pre-order from online catalogs available at carolynsshadegardens.com, and then are picked up in person. The garden is open for viewing by customers and their families and friends only at time of order pick up.

Valley Forge Flowers

503 W. Lancaster Ave., Wayne, PA 19087
610-687-5566
valleyforgeflowers.com

HOURS: Mon.–Sat. 9–5, Sun. 11–4

AMENITIES:

EVENTS: Workshops, cooking classes, trunk shows

Valley Forge Flowers has been a Main Line source for flowers, garden plants, and decorations for more than 50 years. Owner Barbara King's career in horticulture and design began at a very early age, following in the footsteps of her father and grandfather. Under her leadership, Valley Forge Flowers has earned an international reputation for floral and event design that spans the realm from weddings and society events to the Academy of Music's Anniversary Ball and the Philadelphia Flower Show.

Valley Forge Flowers consists of the Flower Shop, the Barn, and the Cottage all located in the Eagle Village Shops plaza. The Flower Shop offers a stunning selection of both fresh and silk flowers and made-to-order floral arrangements. A greenhouse displays seasonal flowering plants and orchids, with an accompanying selection of decorative containers. You will find candles, wreaths, table settings, as wells as designer soaps and creams. The Barn features eclectic furnishings, home decor, and seasonal decorations for both indoor and outdoor living. An outdoor nursery offers a curated selection of shrubs, tropicals, annuals, and perennials for the garden and patio. Beautiful pots, statues, and accessories complement the plant selections. Cafe Fleur and The Cottage Cafe are great stops for lunch or an afternoon treat.

Jenkins Arboretum

631 Berwyn Baptist Rd., Devon, PA 19333
610-647-8870
jenkinsarboretum.org

AREA: 48 acres
HOURS: May 1–Aug. 31: daily 9–8. See website for hours
ADMISSION: Free
AMENITIES:
EVENTS: Plant sale, Spring Blooms Celebration, educational programs

The Jenkins Arboretum is a beautiful natural refuge with a world-class collection of rhododendrons and azaleas. It was once the cherished home and garden of H. Lawrence and Elisabeth Phillipe Jenkins. When Elisabeth passed away in 1963, Lawrence chose to preserve the land as a memorial to his wife. In 1973 neighbor Louisa P. Browning contributed additional property and the arboretum opened to the public in 1976.

Based on the topography, climate, and natural woodlands found on the property, the arboretum decided to focus on native flora as well as plants in the *Ericaceae* (heath) family such as rhododendrons, azaleas, mountain laurels, and blueberries. Located in hardiness Zones 6b/7, the property is ideal for both evergreen azaleas, which grow best further south, and large-leaved rhododendrons,

which flourish further north.

Today, 1.2 miles of paved paths wind through a layered woodland of native oaks and hickories with unique specimens of *Franklinia*, pawpaw, striped maple, buttonbush, and empress tree. Redbuds, fringe trees, Carolina silverbells, American hollies, and sourwoods add seasonal interest with their blooms and berries.

The real stars here are the 5,000 plants in the *Ericaceae* collection, many of which are native and exclusively found at Jenkins Arboretum. Several of these species are extremely rare in the wild and may be lost due to changing environmental conditions and development of natural areas. The arboretum is developing a Native Rhododendron Germplasm Repository to ensure that these northeastern natives are preserved. Some of the natives that you will find here are the white Alabama azalea, the pinkshell azalea, the low-growing coastal azalea , the large-flowered flame azalea, and numerous pink pinxters that grow wild throughout the garden and display an amazing diversity of color and form. Many of the native species are wonderfully fragrant.

Blooming season begins in late March with purple *Rhododendron dauricum* and pink Korean azaleas and ends in late July with the red-orange plumleaf azalea and blush pink rosebay rhododendron. Peak color is in early May, when thousands of rhododendrons, azaleas, and mountain laurels in shades of pale pink, peach, magenta, red, violet, white, purple, and yellow put on a spectacular show. Drifts of bulbs, Virginia bluebells, trilliums, woodland phlox, mayapples, and lady's slipper orchids complement the blooming shrubs and trees. Throughout the rest of the year, other native shrubs and wildflowers continue the floral display and provide interest with their foliage and berries. Large areas of the arboretum are set aside as conservation woodlands.

Jenkins Arboretum, Devon, PA

Terrain

914 Baltimore Pike, Glen Mills, PA 19342
610-459-2400
shopterrain.com

HOURS: Daily 10–6
AMENITIES: 👫 👥 ❌

Also at 138 Lancaster Ave., Devon; 2100 Lower State Rd.,
Doylestown, PA; and 561 Post Road East, Westport, CT

In 2008, the Anthropologie/Urban Outfitters team
bought an 11-acre, 100-year-old garden center
in Glen Mills, and transformed it into Terrain at
Styer's, a garden destination aimed at the "light-
hearted sophisticate"—a hip young customer. The
shop offers stylish home and garden accessories,
furniture and indoor plants. It's a place to meet a
friend to browse for several hours and then enjoy
a leisurely lunch at the farm-to-table cafe.

Among the rustic wares on offer: willow edgers,
stone topiary finials, Nutscene garden twine,
handcrafted pottery, and a large assortment of vases, and terrariums. Orchids, succulents, topiaries,
and tropicals are potted in handsome containers.
All-natural soaps and creams are displayed on

antique sideboards. Modern outdoor furniture,
lighting, and seasonal decor are available for the
discriminating shopper. The nursery yard offers
native plants, annuals, and enough unusual varieties to satisfy the plant connoisseur. The curated
selection and elegant staging provide tons of
inspiration.

Brandywine Cottage

Downington, PA
davidlculp.com

AREA: 2 acres

HOURS: Groups by appointment only, see website

Brandywine Cottage is the private garden of garden designer, author, lecturer, and plant hybridizer David Culp. David is Vice President of Sales and Marketing at Cavano's Perennials. He is a renowned expert and owner of Brandywine Snowdrops, and creator of the Brandywine Hybrid strain of hellebores. His two-acre garden in Downington served as the inspiration for his books, *The Layered Garden* (2012) and *A Year at Brandywine Cottage* (2020).

David has been gardening since childhood thanks to encouragement provided by both sets of grandparents. Descended from a long line of Pennsylvania farmers, he first established a vegetable garden at his 1790s stone farmhouse 30 years ago. Surrounded by double borders of flowers on all sides, the four-square vegetable garden became the heart of his Brandywine Cottage garden–a garden that nourished the body as well as the soul. A neat

white picket fence and double borders of flowers enclose the vegetables, The exuberant plantings create a changing tapestry of color and form. The borders change with the seasons, with alliums, foxgloves, irises, and forget-me-nots in spring followed by lilies, phloxes, patrinia, and Joe Pye weed in summer. Additional beds feature roses underplanted with peonies, euphorbias, geraniums, and catmint. In late summer the bold forms of brugmansias, bananas, and cordylines provide strong architectural interest. David is famous for the snowdrops and hellebores he breeds, and one border is dedicated to hellebores that provide a symphony of color from February to April.

To create interest in the garden all through the year, David and his partner Michael Alderfer use an approach called layered gardening. David describes it as "a design process by which I try to maximize the beauty and interest from each planted space, by combining complementary plants that either grow and bloom together or follow each other in succession." Layered gardening allows them to grow a wide range of plants and enjoy color schemes and plant combinations that change with the seasons.

The hillside garden is a woodland garden that bursts into bloom in spring, with thousands of snowdrops, narcissus, hellebores, and spring ephemerals that flower with magnolias and redbuds. As the deciduous trees leaf out, this becomes a shade garden of hostas, ferns, and many hydrangea varieties that bloom from summer to fall. David's newest project is a naturalistic meadow garden on the east side of the property with native trees, grasses, and wildflowers that will provide a habitat for wildlife. Throughout the gardens you will find collections of rare and unusual plants; pots of clivias, begonias, and orchids; and cozy seating areas. The garden is inviting and inspirational in all seasons.

Scott Arboretum of Swarthmore College

500 College Ave., Swarthmore, PA 19081
610-328-8025
scottarboretum.org

AREA: 300 acres

HOURS: Daily dawn–dusk

ADMISSION: Free

AMENITIES:

EVENTS: Plant sales, lectures, tours, workshops

The Scott Arboretum encompasses the entire campus of Swarthmore College, just seven miles from downtown Philadelphia. It is a series of gardens that showcase more than 4,000 different plants, and was established in 1929 in memory of alumnus Arthur Hoyt Scott. The combination of stately classical architecture and beautiful gardens makes Swarthmore College one of the most attractive college campuses in the United States.

There are 26 distinct garden areas within the Arboretum that can be seen on a self-guided tour lasting about two hours. The trees and shrubs have all been selected for their beauty, ease of maintenance, and resistance to pests and diseases. You

will also find several gardens devoted to native plants. The Arboretum is designed for interest in all seasons. In early spring, the Cherry Border displays 50 types of ornamental cherries suited to the Delaware Valley. More than 150 magnolias peak in the first two weeks of April, followed by lilacs, which formed the first Arboretum collection. In mid-May, you will enjoy the Rhododendron Display Garden. The Tree Peony Collection is also dazzling at this time, with more than 80 varieties, including Japanese and Chinese tree peonies, Itohs, French hybrids and Daphnis hybrids.

One hundred varieties of roses bloom in the Dean Bond Rose Garden from May through frost. Mid-summer is also the best time to enjoy the Theresa Lang Garden of Fragrance and the Pollinator Garden. The Hydrangea Collection steals the show in late summer, followed by the Metasequoia Allée and the Crum Woods in autumn. The Pinetum and Winter Garden are of special interest from November until March, with their striking conifers, winter jasmine, and swaths of hellebores.

Designed by Philadelphia landscape architect Thomas Sears and completed in 1942, the naturalistic outdoor amphitheater provides the backdrop for Swarthmore College's ceremonies. Paths and stone steps wind through the native birch, oaks, and dogwoods of Crum Woods, opening onto the theater, which is built into a steep, natural slope. Screened by holly, oriental spruce, and red cedars, the 220-foot long amphitheater is edged by a low stone wall framed with mature rhododendrons. Eight curving retaining walls, each two feet tall and composed of native schist slabs, descend the 23-foot drop and create terraced, grass-covered seating. Mature tulip poplars and white oaks, spaced randomly, create a canopy above the audience.

For a listing of college arboretums, see page 208.

Tyler Arboretum

515 Painter Rd., Media, PA 19063
610-566-9134
tylerarboretum.org

AREA: 650 acres

HOURS: April–Sept.: Mon.–Fri. 9–6, Sat.-Sun. 8–8; Oct.–Mar.: Mon.–Fri. 9–4, Sat.–Sun. 9–5

ADMISSION: $18

AMENITIES:

EVENTS: Tyler at Twilight, Plant sale in May, hikes

The Tyler Arboretum is a public garden that combines modern sensibilities with a long history. It began with the purchase of a sizable tract of land by English Quaker Thomas Minshall from William Penn in 1681. From 1681 to 1944, the ancestral farm was home to eight generations of the Minshall/Painter/Tyler families. In the early 1800s, brothers Jacob and Minshall Painter collected 1,100 tree, shrub, and herbaceous plant specimens for scientific study. Twenty of those majestic trees

continue to flourish in the arboretum, including a gingko, sweet gum, Yulan magnolia, giant sequoia, and bald cypress. The brothers also built a library for their large collection of books, equipment, and natural science specimens. The Painter Library is one of several historic buildings that remain on the property, along with the 1738 Lachford Hall, which was the family's residence for 200 years and houses original furniture and memorabilia.

In 1944 descendant Laura Tyler bequeathed the property to a board of trustees and it became a nonprofit public garden. Dr. John Caspar Wister was appointed director and with his wife, Gertrude, established the beautiful collections of magnolias, cherries, dogwoods, crabapples, and lilacs that you see today. He created an imposing 85-acre pinetum of hemlocks, pines, firs, spruces, cedars, and larches and a rhododendron collection that displays more than 500 rhododendrons and 200 azaleas.

Tyler's mission is to "conserve our historic landscapes and connect people with the natural world." This includes education through gardening. The central hub for this is Lucille's Garden, with its beautifully planted vegetable garden, surrounded by the children's play area, rain garden, and dry garden. The Pollinator Preserve and four-acre Meadow Maze provide nourishment and habitat for birds, insects, and caterpillars. A wildlife pond and six whimsical treehouses encourage exploration and outdoor play. Pink Hill features a rare ecosystem with its underlying bedrock of serpentine stone and a wildflower meadow abundant with pink creeping phlox. More than 17 miles of hiking trails wind through 550 acres of gardens, meadows, and dense woodlands. Classes, workshops, and themed walks inspire adults and children to learn about nature, horticulture, and botany.

Longwood Gardens

1001 Longwood Rd., Rte. 1, Kennett Square, PA 19348
610-388-1000
longwoodgardens.org

AREA: 1,077 acres total

HOURS: Open year-round Wed.–Mon.: 10–6. Early May–late Oct.: weekends 10–10. See website for details.

ADMISSION: $23

AMENITIES: 👪 🍼 ✖ 🚼

EVENTS: Fountain Shows, music & theater performances, seasonal displays

One of the world's great gardens, Longwood has a history of legacy, innovation, and stewardship. Industrialist Pierre S. du Pont purchased the property in 1906 to save what was then the Pierce

family arboretum from being sold for lumber. Having grown up near Wilmington, Delaware, Pierre had a love for the area's natural beauty, and came from a long tradition of gardeners. His great grandfather established the productive gardens at Hagley, his cousin Henry was a horticulturist and owner of Winterthur, and cousin Alfred built the elegant French gardens at Nemours.

After studying at the Massachusetts Institute of Technology, Pierre joined the family business, DuPont Company, a manufacturer of gunpowder, which had been started by his great-grandfather. Under Pierre's leadership, the company expanded and diversified to become one of the largest corporations in the world.

When he bought the Pierce farm at the age of 36, Pierre had no great plan. He hired a landscape designer but was so disappointed with the results that he decided to design the gardens personally. He built the garden piece by piece, starting with a 600-foot old-fashioned flower border of perennials, biennials, and annuals. Having traveled the world from an early age, Pierre was heavily influenced by the architectural qualities and water features of Italian villa and French chateau gardens. He also was awed by the latest technology, particularly the huge display of water pumps at the 1876 Centennial Exposition in Philadelphia, and the illuminated fountains at the 1893 World's Columbian Exposition in Chicago. He incorporated these features into his gardens, and spared little expense on the construction and mechanical costs of his extensive system of fountains and massive conservatory. Since he had no children, he founded the Longwood Foundation and left most of his estate "for the maintenance and improvement of the gardens."

You will need an entire day to see Longwood Gardens, and then you will want to come back again in a different month. In spring there are jaw-drop-

ping displays of tulips, daffodils, and flowering trees. A highlight in summer is the richly planted Flower Walk with brightly colored annuals and tropicals. In autumn, visit the famous Chrysanthemum Festival and enjoy the quiet beauty of the Meadow Garden with its grasses and native flowers. Winter at Longwood is marked with a magnificent indoor Christmas display, thousands of outdoor lights, and the topiary garden dusted with snow.

Longwood's greenhouses feature amazing displays throughout the seasons. The first was built to grow flowers, vegetables, and grapes. Du Pont created the 1921 Conservatory to showcase fruit and flowers in a decorative, horticultural way. The tradition continues today with dramatic seasonal floral displays. Don't miss the Curving Green Wall with 47,000 plants (25 species of ferns) that create a vertical garden around 17 lavatory cabinets.

Longwood Gardens is renowned for its fountains, which were an awesome feat of engineering when they were installed and continue to amaze visitors today. The five-acre Main Fountain Garden was reopened in 2017 after a $90-million, two-and-a half-year restoration. Hundred of fountains were refurbished, limestone embellishments and stone flowers were crafted by French masons in Wisconsin, and thousands of boxwoods were replanted along the gracious lawns. Set to music, the fountain shows are astonishing by day or night.

An amateur pianist, Pierre loved the performing arts. He constructed the world's largest residential organ for his ballroom and showcased the leading artists of his time. The tradition continues today with a year-round performance series of dance, theater, classical, jazz, and choral music.

Longwood Gardens is currently in the process of completing "Longwood Reimagined," an ambitious expansion which includes the new West Conservatory, Cascade Garden, Bonsai Courtyard, Waterlily Court, restaurant, event spaces, and surrounding landscapes. The Orchid House is already complete, and the rest of the garden spaces are scheduled to open soon.

Hershey Gardens

170 Hotel Rd., Hershey, PA 17033
717-534-3492
hersheygardens.org

AREA: 23 acres

HOURS: Feb.–May: daily 9–5, June–Aug.: daily 9–6

ADMISSION: $16.50

AMENITIES: 👫 🍴 🚼

EVENTS: Orchid Show, adult and family programs

In the 1930s, Milton S. Hershey, philanthropist and founder of the Hershey chocolate company, was asked to sponsor a national rosarium in Washington, D.C. In keeping with his philosophy of supporting the local community, Hershey instead decided to "create a nice garden of roses" in his own town. What began as a 3.5-acre rose garden in 1937 grew to a beautiful botanical garden on 23 acres in five short years.

The Historic Hershey Rose Garden is still the focal point at Hershey Gardens, with 3,500 rose bushes representing 275 varieties of hybrid teas, floribundas, miniatures, shrub roses, and old garden roses. Stepping out of the Visitor Center, the view of Swan Lake flanked by thousands of colorful rose blossoms is spectacular.

A central path leads from the rose garden gazebo to the Seasonal Display Garden, where you will find a dazzling 20,000 tulips in spring, followed by colorful annuals and tropicals in summer and

chrysanthemums in the fall. It continues to the M. S. Hershey Tribute Garden, which commemorated Hershey Gardens' 75th anniversary in 2010. It features the red 'M. S. Hershey' rose, named by the American Rose Society in 1940 and dedicated on Hershey's 83rd birthday. Other themed gardens include a Japanese Garden, Herb Garden, Rock Garden, Ornamental Garden, and Perennial Garden. The themed gardens are framed by groupings and specimens of Japanese maple, dawn redwood, seven-son flower, and weeping cedar. Other unusual trees are featured in the arboretum and the newly planted nut grove.

Hershey Gardens is an excellent destination for small children. Entered through a caterpillar-shaped living tunnel draped in chocolate vine, the 1.5-acre Children's Garden is whimsical, interactive, and educational. A butterfly-shaped pollinator garden, fountains shaped like Hershey's Kisses, the Pretzel Maze, the ABC garden, and 21 other themed gardens offer hands-on fun. The Butterfly Atrium in the conservatory is a year-round attraction, with hundreds of North American and tropical butterflies fluttering through a tropical oasis. Palm trees, ti plants, hibiscus, and even the cacao tree that is used to make chocolate create a beautiful setting for leopard lacewings, Great Mormons, blue morphos, and many other butterflies and moths. A large Chrysalis Cabinet illustrates the butterfly lifecycle from egg to caterpillar, pupa, and adult.

Suggested Daily Itineraries

Hagley Museum, Wilmington (1)
Lunch–Eclipse Bistro, Wilmington
Nemours Estate, Wilmington (3)

Winterthur Museum, Garden & Library, Wilmington (2)
Lunch–Winterthur Cafe, Wilmington
Mt. Cuba Center, Wilmington (4)

Marian Coffin Gardens at Gibraltar, Wilmington (5)
Brandywine Park, Wilmington (6)
Lunch– Big Fish Grill on the Riverfront, Wilmington
Riverfront Wilmington, Wilmington (7)

Amstel House, New Castle (11)
Lunch–Jessop's Tavern, New Castle
Read House & Garden, New Castle (10)

University of Delaware Botanic Garden, Newark (9)
Snack–University of Delaware Creamery

Delaware Botanic Garden at Pepper Creek, Dagsboro (12)
Lunch–Good Earth Market & Restaurant, Ocean View

DELAWARE

Hagley Museum

200 Hagley Creek Rd., Wilmington, DE 19807
302-658-2400
hagley.org

AREA: 235 acres
HOURS: Daily 10–5
ADMISSION: $20
AMENITIES:
EVENTS: Lectures, family events, Holidays at Hagley

Located on 235 acres on the banks of the Brandy-wine River, Hagley is the ancestral home of the du Pont family and the site of the family gunpowder works, restored mills, and a library dedicated to business and technology in America.

Eleuthère Irénée (E. I.) du Pont emigrated to the United States from France in 1799. He founded the gunpowder manufacturing company, and in 1803 he built a Georgian-style home named Eleutherian Mills. The house was surrounded by a garden and a complex of buildings that served as the nucleus of his family and business life. Du Pont was an experienced gardener from his youth and built the garden to feed his family in his isolated Brandywine home. The two-acre home garden is situated in front of the residence and reflects du Pont's original design and plants that were available in the early 1800s. The garden is laid out in a formal parterre pattern with gravel paths and

borders of antique apple, pear, and peach trees. The dwarf pear trees were trained in a conical shape called *en quenouille* that was popular in France in the 1800s. Apple and peach trees were espaliered on fences or grown as horizontal cordons. Du Pont ordered many of his trees, shrubs, and vegetable and flower seeds from France. He supplemented them with native plants obtained from the surrounding woods or from renowned horticulturists such as John Bartram. Beyond the garden was an orchard of more than 100 varieties of pear, apple, peach, plum, and cherry trees.

The garden is beautiful in the spring with the blossoms of the fruit trees, tulips, and groves of purple and white lilacs in the lower end of the garden. In summer you will see Oriental poppies, nasturtiums, zinnias, marigolds, and sunflowers interplanted among heirloom vegetables, as was the custom in the early 1800s. In the fall apples, pears, and pumpkins provide a bountiful harvest. More than 1,500 pounds of produce are donated to local food banks each year.

The second garden on the property is not open to the public but can be viewed from the house terrace. This garden was constructed by the home's last residents, E. I.'s great-granddaughter Louise du Pont Crowninshield and her husband, Francis. Beginning in 1923, the couple spent 10 years creating

a garden on the terraced ruins of the mill that had suffered a major explosion and had been abandoned. Aided by local craftsmen, Francis designed the garden while Louise did the plantings. The design and architectural features were loosely based on the ruin gardens that the Crowningshields visited in Rome. There were cascading layers of Italianate pools, columns, statuary, and colonnades built to look like ancient relics. Enhancing the architectural features was a rich, sophisticated planting scheme borrowed from English gardens.

When the Hagley Museum was created in 1957, many of the architectural elements were taken apart and given away while the garden was left to nature. Today, the garden is in its earliest stages of restoration with stabilization of the architectural elements and clearing of weeds and invasives.

The rest of the Hagley property is a beautiful landscape of woodlands and native shrubs, with canals and the historic remains of the mill buildings and workers compound. It is particularly stunning in fall with the colorful foliage of native trees.

Winterthur Museum, Garden & Library

5105 Kennett Pike, Wilmington, DE 19735
800-448-3883
winterthur.org

AREA: 60 acres of gardens within 1,000-acre estate
HOURS: Spring–Fall: Gardens: Tues.–Sun. 10–5; House tours: Tues.–Sun. 10–3:30, reservations required
ADMISSION: $25
AMENITIES: 🏛️ 🚻 🍴 ❌ 🐾
EVENTS: Point-to-Point, Delaware Antiques Show, Yuletide at Winterthur, Artisan Market, programs, classes

Nestled in 1,000 acres of rolling hills and meadows in the Brandywine Valley, Winterthur is a historic estate with a magnificent 60-acre garden and a museum of American decorative arts. The collection of 90,000 objects made or used in America since 1640 is displayed in a 175-room museum that was once the home of Henry Francis du Pont. Accompanying graduate degree programs and an extensive research library make Winterthur the leading center of decorative arts in the country.

When Henry Francis du Pont inherited Winterthur in 1927, he had already been responsible for its garden for almost 20 years. He had grown up on the estate, which had been in the du Pont family since 1816. The du Ponts had a shared interest in horticulture and farming. At its height, Winterthur was its own town, with 2,500 acres of farms, vegetable and flower gardens, a sawmill, a

railroad station, a post office, and its own zip code. Henry earned a degree in practical agriculture and horticulture so that he could successfully manage the family estate.

Henry had a lifelong passion for gardens and plants. Influenced by the theories of William Robinson and Gertrude Jekyll as well as his visits to gardens throughout Europe, Henry spent almost 60 years working on his gardens. The estate had second-growth oak-chestnut forests, typical of the Brandywine area. American chestnuts, tulip poplars, red maples, hickories, oaks, and American beeches grew in groupings in the woodlands. A trip to England with his father inspired them to add a pinetum of unusual conifers. In 1909 he began ordering spring bulbs by the tens of thousands and having them planted in large drifts throughout the property. Adjacent to the house, the March Bank was planted in a carpet of glory-of-the-snow, crocuses, snowdrops, Siberian squill, winter aconite, and amur adonis that greet early spring. The du Ponts used Winterthur primarily in spring and fall, so these were the important seasons for flowering displays.

When he added a massive nine-story addition to the house to display his collection of antiques and decorative arts, Henry hired his lifelong friend and landscape designer Marian Cruger Coffin to design a new garden that would integrate the house with the landscape. Marian created a series of terraces and a grand central staircase that descend to a rectangular pool with two charming changing pavilions. Shaded by ancient tulip trees, the hillside plantings sloping down to the pool include dogwoods, viburnums, azaleas, and handkerchief trees. Twenty years later she also designed the Sundial Garden as a spring collection of lilacs, quinces, cherries, crabapples, and dogwoods.

Azalea Woods was a garden that Henry worked on for 40 years. When chestnut blight attacked the

Mt. Cuba Center

3120 Barley Mill Rd., Hockessin, DE 19707
302-239-4244
mtcubacenter.org

AREA: 600 acres

HOURS: April–Oct.: Wed.–Sun. 10–6 See website for more details.

ADMISSION: $15

AMENITIES: 👫 👪

EVENTS: Garden tours, many classes and programs

Mt. Cuba Center began as the family home of Lammot and Pamela Copeland du Pont. Lammot was the great-great-grandson of Eleuthère Irénée du Pont and served as DuPont Corporation's president in the 1960s. A nephew of Pierre S. du Pont, founder of Longwood Gardens, he shared the family's love of gardens. The Copelands purchased 127 acres of barren farmland in 1935 and built a brick Colonial Revival manor house. They hired prominent landscape architect Thomas W. Sears to create a walled forecourt, terraces with meadow views, a sweet gum allée, lilac walk, and formal gardens. Twenty years later they worked with Marian Cruger Coffin to add a swimming pool in the shape of a Maltese cross and garden rooms with walkways, flower borders, and outdoor seating.

In the 1960s, the Copelands became increasingly focused on ecology and conservation. Pamela was particularly concerned about the vanishing wildflowers. They purchased additional property with woodlands and a meadow and hired landscape architect Seth Kelsey to develop "wild gardens" with winding paths, ponds, and woodland wildflowers that would contrast with the formal gardens around their home. In the 1970s, already planning on transforming their property into a public botanic garden, they took the advice of University of Delaware professor Dr. Richard W. Lighty to specialize in plants of the Appalachian Piedmont region.

Today Mt. Cuba is home to more than 1,000 species of native plants and center for the study of Appalachian Piedmont flora. Many of these are threatened by extinction in the wild but preserved in the gardens. The center conducts research on the propagation of difficult and underutilized plants so they can be reestablished in their natural landscapes. It also conducts valuable research trials on the best cultivars of native plants for home gardens. Past trials focused on carex, echinacea, phlox, monarda, baptisia, heuchera, hydrangea, and coreopsis, and the results are available on the website. Mt. Cuba has also introduced exceptional new cultivars of native plants.

With native trees and shrubs underplanted with swaths of woodland wildflowers, the gardens at Mt. Cuba are breathtakingly beautiful in spring. Trilliums, lady slippers, foam flowers, woodland phlox, and purple phacelia create carpets of colorful blooms. The meadows burst into bloom in summer with liatrises, lobelias, coreopsis, rudbeckias, and echinaceas. In the fall, woodland asters, solidagos, beautyberry, and winterberry add color with their blooms and berries. The gardens are tranquil, educational, and inspirational. They fulfill their founders' dream of "a place where people will learn to appreciate our native plants and to see how these plants can enrich their lives so that they, in turn, will become conservators of our natural habitats."

Marian Coffin Gardens at Gibraltar

1405 Greenhill Ave., Wilmington, DE 19806
302-322-7100
preservationde.org/marian-coffin-gardens

AREA: 178 acres

HOURS: Daily dawn–dusk

ADMISSION: Free, donations appreciated

Entering the Marian Coffin Gardens at Gibraltar is very much like walking into Frances Hodgson Burnett's *The Secret Garden.* A lush historic walled garden surrounds a dilapidated grand mansion.

When the Gibraltar estate was purchased in 1909 by Hugh Rodney Sharp, an executive at DuPont Corporation, and his wife, Isabella Mathieu du Pont Sharp, sister of Longwood Gardens founder Pierre du Pont, it was already an impressive 19th-century estate. Built in 1884 of Brandywine granite, the mansion was named for the high, rocky outcropping on which it sits. At that time, it included about 80 acres of formal and kitchen gardens, small farm plots, and housing for tenants and staff. The Sharps enlarged the house, adding several wings, a conservatory, swimming pool, and the carriage house that overlooks the parking lot. They lived at Gibraltar for 60 years, raising their three children and enjoying their beautiful garden.

Rodney and Isabella had strong interests in horticulture. Rodney had a greenhouse built above the carriage house where he grew roses, carnations, and other flowers for the house. In 1916 the Sharps hired Marian Cruger Coffin to design the Gibraltar estate gardens in her signature Beaux Arts style. Coffin was a pioneering female landscape architect whose designs are evident at Winterthur, Mt. Cuba, and the University of Delaware. She designed the formal gardens on the property and supervised their installation between 1916 and 1923. Gibraltar's gardens were designed as a series of three terraces leading from the mansion at the top of the rocky hill down to the street level. Each terrace has a unique design and central element, with a wide selection of trees, shrubs, and flowers. Terracing provided a way to navigate the steep slope from the house to the street below. The design of Gibraltar was unusual among gardens of this era. Most mansions had a formal garden adjacent to the house with informal plantings further away. Gibraltar has the opposite, with a naturalistic garden of rhododendrons and woodland trees near the house and formal flower gardens all the way down the slope.

The top flagstone terrace adjacent to the mansion is simple in design and offered a place for the family to relax and enjoy views of the garden below. From there a grand curving marble staircase descended to the evergreen terrace. Designed as a "green garden," the second terrace was planted with southern magnolias, rhododendrons, laurels, and heaths, accented with ferns. It was also the site of the swimming pool, which is now an ornamental water garden.

The bottom terrace was the formal flower garden. It reflects Coffin's unique style: a formal, architectural layout of parallel paths and rectangular lawn, with cottage-style planting beds bursting with flowers. Here you will find blowsy peonies, irises, catmint, rugosa roses, lilies, and gladiolus accented with classical statuary. The centerpiece of the flower garden is a two-tiered marble fountain crowned with a Bathing Venus. From the flower garden, ornate wrought iron gates lead to an allée of bald cypress and azaleas underplanted with English ivy. The allée ends at an Italian-style teahouse with high colonnaded archways.

After Rodney's death in 1968, the mansion was vacant for three decades until it was donated by the family to Preservation Delaware. This organization has restored the gardens and opened them to the public. The future of the mansion remains uncertain with various development proposals under consideration.

Brandywine Park

1080 N. Park Dr., Wilmington, DE 19802
302-577-7020
friendsofwilmingtonparks.org

AREA: 178 acres

HOURS: Daily dawn–dusk

ADMISSION: Free

AMENITIES: 👫 👶

EVENTS: Jasper Crane Rose Garden Party, concerts

Established in 1886 along a mile of the Brandywine River, Brandywine Park is the largest urban park in Delaware. Like other city parks, it originated during the natural landscape movement founded by Frederick Law Olmsted who also consulted on its design.

The park was initially laid out in a naturalistic style with winding paths and roadways framing scenic views of the creek and surrounding woodlands of pin oaks, Norway maples, sweet gums, willows, sycamores, viburnums, laurels, and hollies. In the early 1900s, generous benefactors augmented the arboretum with 150 dogwoods and 100 crabapple trees. In 1929 local attorney J. Ernest Smith donated 114 Japanese flowering cherry trees, which provide a stunning display in early spring. They encircle the Josephine Fountain installed by Smith as a memorial to his wife, Josephine Tatnall Smith, in 1933.

The garden heart of Brandywine Park is the Jasper Crane Rose Garden, created with Public Works Administration funding in 1933. It was established with a donation of 670 roses of 58 varieties by Jasper Crane, an executive of E. I. du Pont de Nemours & Co. The garden was a huge success, proclaimed as "one of the loveliest rose gardens in the country" by the *American Rose Annual* in 1935. It was restored in 2000 with 450 new roses, many donated by rose breeders Conard-Pyle and Jackson & Perkins. The 53 varieties include hybrid teas, floribundas, and climbers that provide a dazzling display from mid-May to October. Volunteers from Friends of Wilmington Parks gather twice weekly to mulch, feed, and prune the roses.

You will also find five Sister Cities flowerbeds at the north end of the Van Buren Street bridge. Sister Cities of Wilmington is an organization formed to promote peaceful relations through cultural exchange. Each of the flower beds is planted in the colors of the national flag of a Sister City: Kalmar, Sweden; Fulda, Germany; Osogbo, Nigeria; Olevano sul Tusciano, Italy; and Nemours, France.

The park also includes the Brandywine Zoo, playgrounds, fitness circuit, athletic fields, and Baynard Stadium.

Riverfront Wilmington

Justison St., Wilmington, DE 19801
302-425-4890
riverfrontwilm.com/directory/riverwalk-hare-pavilion

AREA: 1.3 miles

HOURS: Daily 24 hours

ADMISSION: Free

AMENITIES: 🚻 🧒 ✖ 🍼

EVENTS: Concerts, river tours, many outdoor events

"A river is water in its loveliest form, rivers have life and sound and movement and infinity of variation, rivers are veins of the earth through which the lifeblood returns to the heart."

–Roderick Haig-Brown

There is something so delightful about a city on a river and the resulting combination of urban energy and tranquil nature. Riverfront Wilmington is one of the country's most exciting revitalization stories. Once an industrial wasteland made up of abandoned shipbuilding factories, the Riverfront is now home to a picturesque Riverwalk overlooking the scenic river.

The recently completed 1.3-mile walking path along the Christina River begins at the Tubman-Garrett Riverfront Park and travels to the DuPont Environmental Education Center. You can enjoy inviting restaurants with outdoor dining, take a scenic stroll, bring the kids to Delaware's

Children's Museum, catch a Wilmington Blue Rocks baseball game, rent bicycles, take a cruise on the river, and experience nature at the environmental education center.

The 30-year revitalization process enhanced the landscape bordering the river and restored the ecology of the important environment. A shoreline once strewn with litter and debris is now lush with native plantings and ornamental gardens. More than 27,600 wetland plants were reintroduced to the shoreline, as well as 5,000 trees and shrubs and 36,000 grasses, perennials and annuals. The elevated Riverwalk has been beautifully designed with waterfront benches, statues nestled in the trees, and birdhouses that portray Delaware's prominent buildings. Two industrial cranes reflect the waterfront's shipbuilding history. Drifts of daylilies, roses, blue stars, mallows, hydrangeas, and ornamental grasses line the walkway and provide color from spring through fall.

At the end of the Riverwalk you will find the Russell W. Peterson Urban Wildlife Refuge. Named after a former governor of Delaware who gained international recognition as a scientist and environmentalist, the refuge is 212 acres of freshwater tidal marsh adjoining the Christina River. It is home to the DuPont Environmental Education Center and features exhibits about the area's ecosystem, panoramic river and marsh views, a 10-acre ornamental garden, and a quarter-mile handicap-accessible pond loop extending into the marsh. The refuge is a tranquil sanctuary and home to American bald eagles, wood ducks, beavers, dragonflies, river otters, turtles, and many species of birds. It is also a habitat for a variety of native plants including milkweed, cattail, wild rice, and hibiscus. The refuge is the trailhead for the eight-mile Jack A. Markel rail trail, which follows an abandoned railroad over a bridge and ends at historic New Castle.

The Delaware Center for Horticulture

1810 N. Dupont St., Wilmington, DE 19806
302-658-6262
thedch.org

AREA: 1 acre

HOURS: Daily dawn–dusk

ADMISSION: Free, donations appreciated

AMENITIES:

EVENTS: Lectures, workshops, volunteer opportunities

The Delaware Center for Horticulture (DCH) was formed in 1977 to "inspire individuals and communities through the power of plants." This organization of 600 active and dedicated volunteers has an array of programs designed to cultivate a greener urban community.

DCH is headquartered in the Trolley Square neighborhood of Wilmington on the border of Brandywine Park. The property includes DCH's headquarters building with a 3,000-volume lending library, an art gallery, a lecture hall, and a greenhouse. Surrounding the building is an acre of lush demonstration gardens developed to educate and inspire local gardeners. Walkways and patios illustrate a variety of hardscape materials, including reclaimed bricks and granite blocks that once paved city streets. Pavilions and benches offer places to sit and admire the plantings. The garden is adorned with repurposed structural materials

and local historic artifacts, including a whimsical gate welded from recycled gardening tools and farming equipment, lamp posts that provide support for climbing vines, and classical balustrades from a reconstructed bridge.

The demonstration gardens feature plants that flourish in urban spaces, provide year-round interest, and are locally available in garden centers and nurseries. Ornamental trees such as redbuds, crape myrtles, witch hazels, and paw paws provide structure and seasonal interest with their flowers, fruits, and textured bark. Shade beds display oakleaf hydrangeas, leucothoes, Hakone grass, and other plants that flourish in low-light conditions. Tropicals such as hardy bananas can be grown in Delaware gardens. In the front of the building, a pollinator garden of coneflowers, milkweeds, blue stars, and black-eyed Susans supports local insects and birds. Two interconnected rain gardens illustrate urban ecology and demonstrate the ability of native plants to improve water quality and sustain beneficial pollinators.

The main focus of DCH is the greening of the local community. DCH works with cities and towns to add and maintain public tree plantings. Since its founding, DCH has planted more than 17,000 trees and has trained communities to care for their neighborhood trees. Annual Arbor Day programs teach hundreds of students each year about the importance and care of trees. DCH's Public Landscapes program works with individuals, neighborhoods, governments, and businesses to add plants to challenging urban and suburban environments, from traffic islands and sidewalks to urban meadows and container plantings. Its Urban Agriculture program established the award-winning E. D. Robinson Urban Farm in Wilmington and has provided support for 40 community gardens throughout New Castle County. Through a myriad

of programs, DCH helps to create communities that are healthier, more attractive, and ecologically sustainable.

University of Delaware Botanic Gardens

College of Agriculture and Natural Resources
531 S. College Ave., 152 Townsend Hall, Newark, DE 19716
302-831-0153 canr.udel.edu/udbg

AREA: 15 acres

HOURS: Daily sunrise–sunset

ADMISSION: Free, donations appreciated

AMENITIES: 👥

EVENTS: Tours available, spring plant sale, lectures, winter houseplant sale

The 15-acre University of Delaware Botanic Gardens (UDBG) forms a lush horticultural setting surrounding Townsend Hall, Worrillow Hall, Fischer and South greenhouses, and the UDairy Creamery.

The Emily B. Clark Garden in front of Townsend Hall is the oldest section of UDBG, established in 1973 with funds donated by Emily C. Diffenback, an alumnus and former president of the Delaware Federation of Garden Clubs. It was designed as an ornamental garden and a teaching tool for students. This garden features excellent specimens of woody plants, including paperbark maple, California incense cedar, magnolia 'Leonard Messel,' and golden larch. You will also find collections of dwarf conifers, snowbells, oaks, Japanese maples, and hollies. These are underplanted with large stands of alliums for spring color and amsonias

with their golden foliage for autumn interest.

The Dunham Entrance Garden is a lush shade garden at the south entrance to Townsend Hall. The paved courtyard is shaded by a grand willow oak and sheltered by majestic Japanese cryptomeria and hollies. In spring flowering magnolias create a ceiling of fragrant pink and white petals. Swaths of heucheras, Hakone grass, ferns, Solomon's seal, and persicarias create a colorful tapestry under the woody plants. This garden commemorates Dr. Charles W. Dunham who taught at the university for 30 years and cofounded the botanic gardens with Dr. Richard W. Lighty.

The Herbaceous Garden is a charming display garden as well as an outdoor laboratory for students and researchers. Brick paths wind through flower beds bursting with the blooms of alliums, geraniums, achilleas, and irises in spring; daylilies, daisies, beebalms, and red hot pokers in summer; and sedums, solidagos, asters, and boltonias in fall. This garden is a gateway to the Native Garden, planted with trees, shrubs, and perennials indigenous to the East Coast. Of special interest here is the Lepidoptera Trail, an interpretive garden illustrating beauty and biodiversity in a managed landscape. Lepidoptera is an order of insects including butterflies, moths, and skippers that form a critical link in nature's food web. Based on the research of the University of Delaware's own professor Doug Tallamy, this garden includes more than 50 species of native plants that support many types of Lepidoptera caterpillars and provide nectar for adult insects. Interpretive signs posted along the trail depict the larvae and adults that you may find on the host plants during various months of the year. The trail is an outdoor classroom for gardeners who wish to create beautiful gardens that attract insects and birds.

Other areas of interest include the Trial Gardens, which display new cultivars of annuals, perennials, and tropicals as well as All-American Selections award winners. This award is given to plants that consistently receive high rankings in trial gardens throughout the United States, making them beautiful, adaptable, low-maintenance additions to the home garden. Adjacent to the South Greenhouse is a small garden designed for four-season interest.

Enclosed by a low brick wall lined with deciduous hollies and oakleaf hydrangeas, it is an intimate space. Shrubs with berries, evergreen foliage, and fragrant blooms provide interest throughout the year. Spring daffodils, tulips, grape hyacinths, and leucojums are followed by displays of daylilies, echinaceas, and other summer flowers. In August look for a display of the beautiful and unusual pink resurrection lily (*Lycoris squamigera*).

Read House & Gardens

42 The Strand, New Castle, DE 19720
302-322-8411
readhouseandgardens.org

AREA: 2.5 acres

HOURS: Gardens: daily dawn–dusk; House:
Thurs.–Sun. 11–4

ADMISSION: $10

AMENITIES: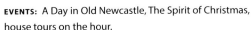

EVENTS: A Day in Old Newcastle, The Spirit of Christmas,
house tours on the hour.

When the Read House was completed in 1803 after six years of construction, it became the largest and grandest home in Delaware for nearly a century. The owner was George Read II, a successful lawyer and businessman, whose father was a signer of the Declaration of Independence, governor of Delaware, and a US senator. Read House faced the Delaware River in downtown New Castle, a bustling shipping town and the capital of Delaware during that time.

Read's 14,000 square-foot brick mansion was built in the high Federal style that swept through Philadelphia in the late 18th century. Read spared no expense in the design, craftsmanship, and materials of his home. He commissioned William Thackara—the plaster artisan who embellished the United States Capitol—to create opulent moldings on his 13-foot ceilings. He installed a huge Palladian window above the entrance and massive parlor doors crafted from Honduran mahogany embellished with custom silver-plated hardware. The home became a showplace the reflected the Reads' status, means, and sophistication.

The gardens at Read House were added by its second owner, William Couper, who purchased the home in 1846. Couper was a wealthy businessman and China tea trader. He expanded the grounds by purchasing adjoining lots and commissioned a renowned Philadelphia nurseryman, Robert Buist, to lay out the gardens. Buist created a garden in three parts: a formal parterre garden adjacent to the house, a naturalistic garden with specimen trees beyond it, and a kitchen garden in the back of the property. Formal "geometric" gardens were popular in the 19th century. Flower beds were divided into square or rectangular plots and subdivided into geometric figures. Boxwood hedges created structure and hearkened back to European knot gardens and parterres.

In 1920 the house was acquired by Philip and Lydia Chichester Laird, both members of the extended du Pont family. The Lairds loved social gatherings and replaced the kitchen garden with a swimming pool and pool house for outdoor entertaining. They also installed a yacht basin at the riverfront. The Lairds were preservationists and instrumental in organizing a community movement to transform New Castle from a fading river town into a charming historic destination. They bequeathed the property to the Delaware Historical Society in 1975.

Today, the gardens surrounding Read House are a celebration of beauty and style within the framework of a mid-19th-century ornamental landscape. Meandering brick walkways accented by white lattice gazebos guide visitors through beds planted with single and double peonies, Siberian

and bearded irises, phloxes, lilies, and hydrangeas. Ornamental shrubs and specimen trees provide multiseason interest with their flowers and foliage. An extensive reinterpretation of the grounds with a revitalized landscape is currently in the works.

Amstel House Museum

2 E. 4th St., New Castle, DE 19720
302-322-2794
newcastlehistory.org

AREA: 1 acre

HOURS: April–Dec.: Thurs.–Sat. 10–4, Sun. 12–4

ADMISSION: $7.50 (Museum tickets are available at the New Castle Visitor Center at the Arsenal, 30 Market St.)

AMENITIES:

EVENTS: Hearth cooking, Halloween events

An elegant brick mansion, Amstel House is one of New Castle's few surviving early colonial buildings. Set on a corner lot on New Castle's main street, the house has a lovely Colonial Revival garden hidden behind its impressive brick walls.

Amstel House was built in the 1730s by the town's wealthiest landowner, Dr. John Finney, an Irish physician and uncle to Declaration of Independence signer Thomas McKean. Its interior is graced with fine architectural details including an early fanlight, central hallway, original woodwork, and an open hearth. In the late 1700s, it was the home of Nicholas Van Dyke, a Revolutionary and the seventh governor of Delaware. Later it belonged to Kensey Johns who was a member of the committee that ratified the Constitution, making Delaware "The First State" in 1787. Today, the house is furnished with many of the Van Dykes' and Johnses' personal possessions.

After a succession of owners in the 19th and early 20th centuries, Amstel House faced an uncertain future. In 1931 a group of concerned citizens raised funds to purchase the property to protect New Castle's historic heritage. The group evolved into the New Castle Historical Society, which has since collaborated with the city and other civic organizations to save, preserve, and restore many of the town's historic architectural treasures.

The garden at Amstel House was designed in the 1930s by renowned landscape architect Charles Gillette who specialized in Colonial Revival gardens. He designed a garden with a brick perimeter wall inspired by walls built in Delaware in the 1700s with stone foundations and sandstone caps. Within the walls, the garden was laid out in three garden rooms, separated by brick walls or hedges and accented with trellises and arbors.

The parterre garden is a formal ornamental garden outlined with herringbone brick paths and boxwood hedges. Seen from above, the paths form the outline of a butterfly. The parterre sections are planted with spring tulips and summer annuals. The lawn garden features a hackberry tree that was planted in 1934 and is one of Delaware's largest specimens. It shades the Garden House, which is a facsimile of a Virginia Georgian tool house that was built using period materials salvaged from other structures. The stepping stones behind the hackberry tree form the Path to Independence and came from the homes of the signers of the Declaration of Independence and other historic sites related to the Revolutionary War. From this path a brick walk marks the edge of the Rear Garden, which features PJM rhododendrons, cherry laurels, boxwoods, and perennials.

In 2018 the garden was renovated by the Arasapha Garden Club in conjunction with landscape architect Anne Walters. The club continues to plant and maintain the garden to this day.

Delaware Botanic Gardens at Pepper Creek

30220 Piney Neck Rd., Dagsboro, DE 19939
302-321-9061
delawaregardens.org

AREA: 37 acres

HOURS: March–Nov.: Thurs.–Sun. 9–4

ADMISSION: $15

AMENITIES:

EVENTS: Tours, workshops, Sea Witch Festival

Located close to the Delaware beaches, the Delaware Botanic Gardens at Pepper Creek is the newest public garden in the state. It was founded in 2012 by a group of Sussex County residents who share a passion for horticulture and it opened to the public in 2019. Situated on 37 acres along Pepper Creek, the garden is an oasis of flowers and grasses, natural wetlands, and woods that are home to birds, pollinators, and other wildlife.

The half-acre Rhyne Garden welcomes you in the parking lot with 'Brandywine' red maple trees underplanted with 300 native shrubs, 12,000 flowering plants, and 86,000 spring bulbs. Beautiful in design, this garden serves an important function in stormwater management. Its central swale collects water runoff from the parking lot, and the plant roots of water-tolerant rose mallows and soft rush serve as natural rain filters that clean the water as it is absorbed. Pollinator plants including coneflower, wild indigo, bee balm, and phlox

stabilize the soil on the slopes.

Sited on an upland plateau, the spectacular two-acre meadow garden is the jewel of the property. Designed by internationally acclaimed Dutch plantsman Piet Oudolf in his signature prairie meadow style, this garden begins blooming with alliums, achilleas, baptisias, and penstemons in spring and provides a stunning display through late fall. Peak bloom time is in late summer, when coneflowers, heleniums, milkweeds, phloxes, and liatrises provide a myriad of textures and colors. Originally planted with 85% native plants, the meadow has matured into a vibrant ecosystem. As flourishing plants self-seeded, they have created a beautiful tapestry that provides food and habitat for bees, butterflies, and birds.

Adjacent to the meadow is the Folly Garden built on the site of a former 20th-century farmhouse. Planters, old fences, and retaining walls recall residents who once called this garden home. Drifts of spring bulbs, hellebores, columbines, and ferns create an intimate garden space. The Learning Garden serves as an outdoor wetland classroom encircling a small pond. The Woodland Garden is a 12.5 -acre riparian forest with freshwater wetlands on the banks of Pepper Creek. Mosses, ferns, and spring ephemerals flourish under the canopy of sweet gums, oaks, loblolly pines, American hollies, and sassafras. A walkway leads to the Knoll Garden, the highest point on the property, with a splendid view of Pepper Creek and the animals that call it home.

A true community endeavor, the Delaware Botanic Gardens continues to grow and mature. Fifteen volunteers form its governing board and hundreds of volunteers plant, weed, and maintain the gardens. From Girl Scout troops to college students, professors, local nurseries, and corporate sponsors, this is a unique, inspirational garden that is supported and cherished by its community.

Visiting Tips

GARDEN TOURING PACKING LIST

- ○ GPS/Maps
- ○ Phone/camera
- ○ Small notebook for recording ideas and plant names
- ○ Water and snacks: many places do not have dining options
- ○ Membership cards to gardening organizations. Some gardens participate in reciprocal admission programs.
- ○ Umbrella and rain gear
- ○ Sun glasses, hat and sunscreen
- ○ Sturdy walking shoes; waterproof shoes are best during morning visits
- ○ Trunk liner for unexpected plant purchases

Longwood Gardens, Kennett Square, PA

GARDEN TOURING ETIQUETTE

Unlike public parks, gardens are designed for plant appreciation, not active recreation. Please use the following guidelines when visiting public or private gardens and nurseries:

✤ Smoking, fire and alcohol are generally not permitted on the premises.

✤ Leave pets, except service dogs, at home.

✤ Do not pick flowers, fruits, or plants.

✤ To protect the plant collections, active sports or games such as frisbee, bicycling, jogging, rollerblading, skating, ball-playing, and kites are generally not permitted in gardens.

✤ Do not walk in the flower beds, climb trees, or wade in ponds or water features.

✤ Deposit trash and recyclables in designated receptacles.

✤ Picnickers are usually welcome—check to see where tables are located.

✤ Silence your cell phones and leave radios at home. Consider your visit as an opportunity to escape from technological intrusions.

✤ Check in advance to see if organized gatherings and private events are permitted on the grounds.

✤ When photographing the garden, do not step into or place tripods in garden beds and respect the wishes of other visitors.

Eating, Shopping and Special Interest Gardens

Terrain, Glen Mills, PA

BEST EATERIES

Adams Fairacre Farm
Grounds for Sculpture
Longwood Gardens
New York Botanical Garden
Terrain
University of Delaware Creamery
Winterthur Museum, Garden &
  Library

BEST GIFT SHOPS

Grounds for Sculpture
Hortulus Farm Garden & Nursery
Longwood Gardens
Lyndhurst
Morris Arboretum & Gardens of the
  University of Pennsylvania
New York Botanical Garden
Olana State Historic Site
Terrain
The Mutter Museum at The College
  of Physicians of Philadelphia

Valley Forge Flowers
Winterthur Museum, Garden &
  Library

WHERE TO BUY PLANTS

Adams Fairacre Farms
Bartram's Garden
Bowman's Hill Wildflower Preserve
Carolyn's Shade Gardens
Holland Ridge Farms
Hortulus Farm Garden & Nursery
Jenkins Arboretum
Longwood Gardens
New York Botanical Garden
Peony's Envy
RareFind Nursery
Stonecrop Gardens
Terrain
The Gardens at Mill Fleurs
Valley Forge Flowers

EARLY SPRING GARDENS

Bowman's Hill Wildflower Preserve
Carolyn's Shade Garden
Chanticleer
Clermont State Historic Site
Holland Ridge Farms
Leonard J. Buck Garden
Longwood Gardens
Mt. Cuba Center
New York Botanical Garden
Stonecrop Gardens
The Gardens at Mill Fleurs
Wave Hill
Willowwood Arboretum
Winterthur Museum, Garden &
  Library

EARLY AUTUMN GARDENS

Chanticleer
Kykuit
Longwood Gardens
New York Botanical Garden

Kykuit, Pocantico Hills, NY

Stonecrop Gardens
Willowwood Arboretum

ROSE GARDENS
Brandywine Park
Colonial Park Rose Garden
Deep Cut Gardens
Hershey Gardens
Center City Philadelphia Gardens
Kykuit
Longwood Gardens
Lyndhurst
New York Botanical Garden
Scott Arboretum of Swarthmore
    College
Springwood
Vanderbilt Estate
Wyck
Yaddo Garden

HERB GARDENS
Boscobel

Montgomery Place
The Mutter Museum at The College
    of Physicians of Philadelphia
New York Botanical Garden
Northview
The Met Cloisters

VEGETABLE GARDENS
Chanticleer
Hagley Museum
Longwood Gardens
New York Botanical Garden
Rutgers Gardens
Springwood
Stonecrop Gardens
Tyler Arboretum

ALPINE GARDENS
Chanticleer
Leonard J. Buck Garden
New York Botanical Garden
Stonecrop Gardens

RHODODENDRONS/AZALEAS
Jenkins Arboretum
Laurelwood Arboretum
Leonard J. Buck Garden
Mt. Cuba Center
Morris Arboretum & Gardens of the
    University of Pennsylvania
New York Botanical Garden
Rare Find Nursery
Shofuso Japanese Garden
Tyler Arboretum
Van Vleck House and Gardens
Winterthur Museum, Garden &
    Library

GREENHOUSES
Deep Cut Gardens
Duke Farms
Hershey Gardens
Longwood Gardens
New York Botanical Garden
Stonecrop Gardens
Wave Hill

TOURING WITH CHILDREN

Public gardens can introduce children to the beauty and variety of the plant world. Many gardens feature children's gardens, provide activity backpacks, or host special family visiting days. Young children can be entertained with activity books, drawing supplies, and games—I Spy, Hide & Seek, and identification games. I found that when my kids were older, they enjoyed picnics, drawing, watercolor painting, photography, and looking for wildlife—birds, frogs, lizards, and fish—in the gardens. Binoculars and magnifying glasses were good accessories. A cooler of snacks and drinks was always a necessity.

Gardening Organizations and Events

PRESERVATION ORGANIZATIONS

Garden State Gardens
gardenstategardens.org

Greater Philadelphia Gardens
americasgardencapital.org

Hudson River Valley Heritage Area
hudsonrivervalley.com

National Trust for Historic Preservation
savingplaces.org

The Garden Conservancy
gardenconservancy.org

HORTICULTURAL SOCIETIES

American Horticultural Society
ahsgardening.org

Delaware Native Plant Society
delawarenativeplants.org

Hardy Plant Society/Mid-Atlantic
hardyplant.org

New Jersey State Horticultural Society
njshs.org

Pennsylvania Horticultural Society
phsonline.org

The Delaware Center for Horticulture
thedch.org

The Horticultural Society of New York
thehort.org

GARDEN CLUB FEDERATIONS

Delaware Federation of Garden Clubs
delawaregardenclubs.org

Federated Garden Clubs of New York State
fgcnys.com

Garden Club Federation of New Jersey
gardenclubofnewjersey.com

Garden Club Federation of Pennsylvania
pagardenclubs.org

National Garden Clubs
gardenclub.org

FLOWER AND GARDEN SHOWS

Capital District Garden & Flower Show
March, gardenandflowershow.com

Macy's Flower Show
March-April, visitmacysusa.com/event/macys-flower-show

Philadelphia Flower Show
March, phsonline.org

FLOWER FESTIVALS

Albany Tulip Festival
May, albany.com/things-to-do/tulip-festival/

Chrysanthemum Festival, Longwood Gardens
October–November, longwoodgardens.org

Daffodil Celebration, New York Botanical Garden
May, nybg.org

Holland Ridge Farms Tulip Festival
April, hollandridgefarm.com

Lewes Tulip Celebration
April, leweschamber.com

Mt. Cuba Wildflower Weekend
April, mtcubacenter.org

Orchid Show, The New York Botanical Garden
February-April, nybg.org

Rose Weekend, New York Botanical Garden
June, nybg.org

Resources

A Year at Brandywine Cottage: Six Seasons of Beauty, Bounty and Blooms
David Culp

Always Growing: The Story of the Morris Arboretum
Christine Pape, editor

Andalusia: Country Seat of the Craig and Biddle Family
Nicholas Wainwright

Beatrix Farrand: Private Gardens, Public Landscapes
Judith B. Tankard

Du Pont Gardens of the Brandywine Valley
Larry Lederman, Marta McDowell

Gardens of the Garden State
Nancy Berner and Susan Lowry

Gardens of the Hudson Valley
Nancy Berner and Susan Lowry

Glorious Shade
Jenny Rose Carey

Great Gardens of America
Tim Richardson

Longwood Gardens: 100 Years of Garden Splendor
Colvin Randall

Marian Coffin Gardens at Gibraltar
Erin Fogarty, Dr. Jules Bruck

Mt. Cuba
Rick J. Lewandowski & Jeanne Frett

Nature into Art: The Gardens of Wave Hill
Thomas Christopher

Rescuing Eden: Preserving America's Historic Gardens
Caroline Seebohm

Shakespeare's Flowers
Jessica Kerr

The Art of Gardening: Design Inspiration and Innovative Planting Techniques from Chanticleer
R. William Thomas

The Brother Gardeners
Andrea Wulf

The Layered Garden: Design Lessons for Year-Round Beauty from Brandywine Cottage
David Culp

The New York Botanical Garden
Gregory Long & Anne Shellin, editor

The Rockefeller Family Gardens: An American Legacy
Larry Lederman, Cynthia Bronson Altman, Todd Forrest

The Ultimate Flower Gardener's Guide
Jenny Rose Carey

The Winterthur Garden: Henry Francis du Pont's Romance with the Land
Denise Magnani

Garden Index

Photo credits

All photography by Jana Milbocker except for:

Locust Grove Estate: 32, 33. Tamara Monson: 40. Littleny: 55. New York Botanical Garden: 61 top, 63. Laurelwood Arboretum: 68 middle. Claire Stapleton: 75 bottom. Reeves-Reed Arboretum: 80, 81. Moira Keihm: 84 bottom, 85 top. Lauren Errickson: 85 bottom right. Peony's Envy: 88, 89. Duke Farms: 97 top & left. Richard Speedy, courtesy of Morven House & Gardens: 99 top. Deep Cut Gardens: 102 bottom, 103 top. RareFind Nursery: 109 bottom. Holland Ridge Farms: 110, 111. Bowman's Hill Wildlife Preserve: 119 top. The Mutter Museum at The College of Physicians of Philadelphia: 132 bottom. Laurel Hill Cemeteries: 137-139. Morris Arboretum & Gardens: 140 top, 141 top. Rob Cardillo Photography: 141 bottom, 142 bottom, 143 top, 165 top. William Rein, The Barnes Arboretum, 145 top & bottom right. Highlands Mansion & Gardens: 146 bottom right, 147 top left. Jenny Rose Carey: 150 bottom, 151. David Korbonits: 152 bottom, 153. Scott Arboretum of Swarthmore College: 166 bottom, 167 top. Tyler Arboretum: 169 middle. Katrina Milbocker: 191 top. The Delaware Center for Horticulture: 195 bottom left. Voxinferior: 198 bottom. Ann Berry: 199 bottom right. Arasapha Garden Club: 201. Stephen Pryce Lea: 202 bottom. Ray Bojarski: 203

New York Botanical Garden, Bronx, NY